The Open University
Arts: a third level course
History of architecture and design 1890–1939
Units 21–22

Unit 21 Mechanical Services

Prepared by Reyner Banham for the Course Team

Unit 22 The Modern Flat

Prepared by Stephen Bayley for the Course Team

The Open University Press

The Open University Press,
Walton Hall, Milton Keynes, MK7 6AA.

First published 1975.

Designed by the Media Development Group of the Open University.

Printed in Great Britain by
Martin Cadbury, a specialized division of Santype International,
Worcester and London.

ISBN 0 335 00710 4

This text forms part of an Open University course. The complete list of units in the course appears at the end of this text.

For general availability of supporting material referred to in this text, please write to the Director of Marketing, The Open University, P.O. Box 81, Walton Hall, Milton Keynes, MK7 6AT.

Further information on Open University courses may be obtained from the Admissions Office, The Open University, P.O. Box 48, Walton Hall, Milton Keynes, MK7 6AB.

1.1

Unit 21 Contents

General Introduction to Units 21 and 22

Units 21 and 22 have been conceived as a corrective to the view that the form of buildings is dictated solely by artistic or aesthetic decisions. Of course, it has been necessary throughout the rest of the units to concentrate on individual architects and the famous buildings which they designed, but we want to suggest here that other factors have moulded the shape of twentieth-century architecture.

In Unit 21 Reyner Banham argues that mechanical services (heating; lighting; lifts and air conditioning) have made possible the formal and stylistic innovations of modern architecture which have hitherto been considered to be solely the products of aesthetic decisions. In Unit 22 Stephen Bayley outlines the real effects of the impact of modern architecture and mechanical services on the life-style of ordinary people by examining the evolution of the flat as a solution to the housing problem.

Units 21 and 22 have been juxtaposed because they both offer an unconventional perspective on the development of modern architecture. Reyner Banham concentrates on the 'High Art' of modernism—he writes of such famous architectural ikons as the Philadelphia Saving Funds Society Building of Howe and Lescaze, of the Maison Dalsace of Chareau and Bijvoet or the Pavillon Suisse by Le Corbusier—but his point of view is unorthodox. He has abandoned nice discussions of style or artistic intent and instead has described in what degree these buildings were formed by the inclusion of mechanical servicing equipment in their specification and has assessed their environmental success.

Similarly, in Unit 22 Stephen Bayley considers the development of the flat not as a response to innovatory styles but as a product of social, political and legislative factors. The flat should have been the flagship of modernism in England but, through a combination of associationism and innate conservatism, never really created a stylistic identity of its own. Indeed, throughout the period of innovation in the 1930s no one style was established as the right one for flats and the case studies in Unit 22 illustrate the diversity of examples with CIAM purity on the one hand, Viennese moderne and English brick-built flats on the other. This stylistic variety suggests some of the ideological instability beneath the impressive propagandizing for flat building and, in the same period when mechanical services were beginning to make a real impact on architecture, this perspective on an aspect of the ferment in architecture seems to be appropriate.

AIMS OF UNITS 21 AND 22

The purpose of these two units is:

1 To show the extent to which mechanical services have moulded the form of buildings.

2 To explain which architects were able to incorporate mechanical services into their buildings and how this affected the form.

3 To analyse the increasing importance of mechanical services in the design of building.

4 To show that in the nineteenth century a systematic new form of housing evolved and became the twentieth century's solution to the housing shortage.

5 To show that even the most modest flats built after *c.* 1930 incorporated servicing equipment.

6 To ask whether an identifiable form for the type 'flat' ever evolved.

7 To assess the degree of political and legislative influence on flat design.

8 To investigate the source for the desire for flats as a solution to the housing shortage in the ideology of the Modern Movement.

9 To identify some of the main features of English flat design.

SET BOOKS

Because Units 21–22 chart some little-known waters the material contained in them is not well supported by any of the set books. You will not be asked to read any passages from the set books throughout these two units but it should be useful, however, to have with you the following books to act as controls against which the unconventional history described in these units can be judged:

Hitchcock, H. R., *Architecture: Nineteenth and Twentieth Centuries*, The Pelican History of Art, Penguin, 1971, and Pevsner, N., *Pioneers of Modern Design*, Penguin, 1972.

Both Le Corbusier's *Towards a New Architecture* (trans. F. Etchells) Architectural Press, 1970, and H. R. Hitchcock's and P. Johnson's *The International Style*, W. W. Norton, New York, 1966, are useful as contemporary sources for much of the material and attitudes described in these units, and the A305 Course Anthology, *Form and Function*, ed. C. A. and T. J. Benton with Dennis Sharp, Crosby Lockwood Staples/The Open University Press, 1975, is an invaluable source of documentary and contemporary material by authors and architects cited throughout these units.

RECOMMENDED READING

Banham, R., *The Architecture of the Well-tempered Environment*, Architectural Press, 1970, contains developments of the material of Unit 21.

Jackson, A., *Politics and Architecture*, Architectural Press, 1971, is very useful background reading for Part Four.

Pawley, M., *Architecture versus Housing*, Studio Vista, 1971, is an articulate and stimulating discussion of housing in the twentieth century which offers some valuable insights into problems raised in Unit 22.

Ravetz, A., *Model Estate*, Croom Helm, 1974, is a detailed sociological discussion of the success and failure of the Quarry Hill Estate in Leeds.

Sharp, D., *A Visual History of Twentieth Century Architecture* Heinemann/Secker and Warburg, 1972, is a useful book to have to hand while reading both these units.

Sutcliffe, A. (ed.), *Multi-storey Living*, Croom Helm, 1974, contains a collection of essays (which have a bias towards sociology) concerned with the problems of high-rise blocks.

All the above books should be available in public libraries. The following books and articles will be less accessible but are well worth pursuit.

Flats, Ascot Gas Water Company Ltd., London, 1938.

Denby, E., *Europe Re-housed*, George Allen and Unwin, 1938.

Yorke, F. R. S. and Gibberd, F., *The Modern Flat*, Architectural Press, 1937.

Chambers, H. F. and Soissons, L. de, 'Working Class Housing in Europe', *The Builder*, May 3rd, 1935, pp. 835–6; May 10th, 1935, pp. 861–2.

Ermers, M., 'Housing Policy in Vienna', *Town and Country Planning*, vol. 9, 1941–2, pp. 138–140.

Grieve, A., 'Isokon', *Hampstead in the Thirties—a Committed Decade*, Hampstead Artists' Council Ltd., 1974, pp. 10–24.

Kunze, H., 'Kommunaler Wohnungsbau in Wien der 20er Jahre', *Bauwelt*, March 31st, 1969, pp. 44–9.

Schlandt, J., 'Die Wiener Superblocks 1922–34', *Werk*, vol. 57, April 1970, pp. 221–256.

Wornum, G. G., 'Modern Flats', *Journal of the R.I.B.A.* May 1931, pp. 435–455.

BROADCAST PROGRAMMES

Television Mechanical Services in the Cinema

In this programme Stephen Bayley takes the cinema as the paradigm of mechanical servicing in architecture. One particular cinema is singled out for detailed analysis —the Astoria, Finsbury Park, London. The role of the heating and electrical plant which, in conjunction with the bizarre decoration, combined to produce an emotional and physical atmosphere which was, for many people, their first taste of the convenience and benefits which modern architecture could being, is described in detail. The degree to which mechanical servicing was employed in cinemas (it was a major commercial attraction) anticipated the later application of heating, ventilation and elaborate lighting to more everyday buildings.

Radiovision The Reform of the Skyscraper

The evolution of the skyscraper in America was closely linked to the development of the essential mechanical and electrical services. In this programme Professor Reyner Banham uses the example of the skryscraper to show the importance of mechanical services in architecture.

Radiovision The Work of Isokon

Jack Pritchard was a founder and director of Isokon, and commissioned Wells Coates to design the Isokon Flats in Lawn Road, Hampstead, in the early thirties. Here he talks about the period and illustrates examples of the work of Isokon, particularly in the field of furniture design.

AUTHORS' ACKNOWLEDGEMENTS

Reyner Banham, Professor of the History of Architecture at the School of Environmental Studies, University College, London, wrote Unit 21. Stephen Bayley wrote Unit 22. The authors would like to acknowledge the helpful comments and criticisms which they have received from the Course Team during the preparation of these units.

Part one The Background to Environmental Control

1 Energy sources and services

The building which has been chosen to close and sum up the period covered by this unit is the Secretariat Tower of the United Nations Headquarters [**Plate 1**] in New York, completed in 1950. Its style and format bring together various trends from the thirties which had become accepted as norms of 'progressive' architectural thought not only among architects but among most western intellectuals as well. This late version of the International Style had therefore been adopted by the victorious allies of World War II, who then constituted the only permitted members of the United Nations, as symbolically appropriate to their aspirations for a peaceful, fascist-free, welfare-oriented world.

The basic *parti* of a tall rectangular, glass-walled office slab with an assembly hall or auditorium at its foot surrounded by a public garden, had already appeared, of course, in precisely this role of liberal symbolism in the famous building for the Ministry of Health and Education in Rio de Janeiro, Brazil [**Plate 3**], 1937–43, designed by a team headed by Lucio Costa and Oscar Niemeyer, with Le Corbusier as a consultant.

The design for the UN headquarters was, however, nominally the work of a large team of distinguished architects from the leading allied states, with Wallace K. Harrison as executive architect. The office-tower for the Secretariat was a rectangular thirty-nine-storey slab, clad in stone panelling on its short end-walls, and in high quality total glazing on its two main façades [**Plate 2**]. This form was clearly descended from the pre-war ministry in Rio, and from several generations of sketches by Le Corbusier. The last of these, specifically for the UN headquarters, was turned into a model by Le Corbusier himself—*Project 23A* in Wallace Harrison's New York office in 1946–7 [**Plate 4**].

Le Corbusier himself was not a member of the Design Commission, but when the final design of the Commission was unveiled, its derivation from *Project 23a* was so obvious that accusations of plagiarism inevitably followed. But in the strongly worded letters of complaint which Le Corbusier immediately dispatched to all the leading architectural periodicals in the world, he complained also that he had been unintelligently plagiarized, and that his ideas had been so misunderstood that the building would be uninhabitable (see Appendix 1).

The substance of this subsidiary complaint is that the design showed no sun-shading—*brise-soleils* in Le Corbusier's terminology— on the main glazed façades. These devices usually took the form of a projecting egg-crate or grille of fixed or adjustable members (on the Ministry at Rio, the horizontal members could be adjusted manually) to shade the glass and the interior from the hottest sun, usually at mid-afternoon. As one of the most impassioned proponents of all-glass walls (the *pan de verre*) in the twenties and thirties, Le Corbusier had been forced to invent (or re-invent) such sun-shades himself (see Part 2, section 1 below) and now regarded them as an essential element of the glass-wall concept [**Plate 5**].

Given all-glass walls facing nearly due east and west in a climate such as that of New York, such sun-shades sound no more than good sense; the heat gain from sunlight through glass can be considerable—hence the horticulturalist's greenhouses—and with high air temperatures and high humidity (which normally occur together in the New York summer) could have made conditions in the Secretariat intolerable. How could Harrison and the Commission propose to do without sunshading of some sort? [**Plate 6**]

The answer lies in the work of another great master of the twentieth-century environment, but whose name—Willis Havilland Carrier—appears in none of the standard histories of modern architecture. He took even greater pride in the UN Secretariat than did Le Corbusier, for it was his masterpiece too. He made the architectural conception habitable by designing and installing the most sophisticated and self-effacing system of air-conditioning devised up till then—and as the virtual inventor of air-conditioning, Carrier was still the only man in the world who could have done it. Given his installation, which could generate a cooling effect equivalent to the melting of 2,300 tons of ice, and venetian blinds behind every square inch of glass, the Secretariat tower was habitable without a *brise-soleil*, whatever Le Corbusier might say.

Carrier (born 1876) was almost a decade older than Le Corbusier, and lived just long enough to see the Secretariat finished. The two men did meet at the opening of the building (or so the story has it) but had nothing of interest to say to one another. This was hardly surprising—in spite of Le Corbusier's flurries of interest in various forms of mechanical ventilation, he and Carrier must be seen as representing diametrically opposed views of the management of the human environment: Le Corbusier by modernizing traditional forms of massive construction and permanent shelter, Carrier by the application of mechanical energy almost irrespective of the nature of the building structure.

Many architects of their generation were conscious of the possible threat to their traditional position that the mechanical and electrical engineers men constituted, and overt hostility did occasionally appear, as when Frank Lloyd Wright boasted, in connection with the Johnson Wax Building, Racine, 1936 (see Units 7–8, Plate 72), 'I fired seven engineers, young man, before we were through'. Certainly, by the middle thirties, when the first buildings began to appear in which mechanical and electrical installations accounted for half their total cost (Radio City, New York, or Broadcasting House in London,

Plates 36 and **45**, see Part 2, section 3 below) it could be argued that architects were only half-designers of such buildings, and their traditional dominance as the main creative force in building-design had been seriously eroded.

Mechanical and electrical services are intruders in what might be termed the 'culture of architecture', they are new, since they barely existed before about 1850, whereas the structural side of architecture is as old as civilization itself. Nevertheless, we should not forget that there has never been an architecture in which the consumption of energy—at least for heating, lighting and cooking—was not significant, however small its quantity. *Hearth* is one of oldest synonyms for *Home*.

1 Read Le Corbusier's letter to Senator Warren Austin (reproduced as Appendix 1). What does this tell you about Le Corbusier's ideas in the field of sun-heat control?

2 Now, as a check on your own usual attitudes and perceptions, make a check of your own immediate environment, first your own room, then the whole building, What do you notice about its servicing provisions?

● 1 Note that it makes no mention of air-conditioning, and that it mistakes or misquotes Wallace Harrison's intentions making it appear that he plagiarized Le Corbuser's *mur neutralisant* (discussed further in Part 2, Section one, below). Carrier was already at work on the air-conditioning installation, of which the editors of at least one American magazine must have known, yet none of those who reprinted the letter raised the point. The whole affair shows how prone we are to think of architecture in ways that exclude its energy-consuming aspects.

2 You should have noticed how much of its heat and light comes from 'natural', how much from 'industrial' sources, how does the air you breathe enter the space you are in; how many gas and electricity outlets are there; how many abandoned or disused outlets are there (they are witness to the industrial archaeology of your surroundings); how many appliances does the household boast that consume power—not forgetting that some may carry their power with them in the form of batteries, paraffin, clockwork. If you are a householder, how much of your weekly budget goes on environmental power (gas, electricity, coal, oil) and how much on environmental structure (rent or mortgage payments). Now find someone in his eighties and compare notes about his earliest memories of the domestic environment! ●

The date of 1850 as the historical breakpoint between old and new methods of deploying environmental power is a very approximate one. It has more to do with methods of distribution than with any new inventions of equipment. Thus the invention of the relatively clean-burning oil lamp with controllable wick (flat wick, 1780 approximately, tubular wick 1838), in a glass chimney, made little difference until cleaner types of oil could be supplied to users, and that had to wait until the development of paraffin and kerosene in the middle of the last century. Again, the use of coal-gas for lighting had been demonstrated around 1800 by Philippe Lebon in Paris and William Murdock in Birmingham [**Plates 8–9**], but remained a very messy affair until F. A. Winzer's proposal to distribute gas from central works was taken up. Manufacture in central gasworks and distribution by public mains did not begin till 1814 in London, and it was to be another three decades before every major settlement in Britain could boast a gasworks.

Gas

In spite of this long-range distribution, gas was still in one way an old-fashioned source of energy—a flame still had to be burned at the place to be heated or lit. By comparison, the less spectacular method of heating by piped steam or hot water (James Watt, appropriately, had his office heated by piped steam in 1784) is a more radical concept. Like its remote ancestor the Roman hypocaust (underfloor hot-air heating), it enabled fuel to be burned at one point and the heat to be delivered elsewhere, but without the accompanying smoke, ash and other pollutants.

Nevertheless, the advantages of gas over most other energy sources were impressive. It was far less messy and far brighter than most other light sources. Though dangerous, it was convenient; and when gas cookers became more generally available after 1860 it became the characteristic source of domestic power for the rest of that century and for much of the present one. Its useful life was greatly extended by the invention of the incandescent mantle by Auer von Welsbach [**Plate 10**] at the beginning of the eighties. Until then, gas had produced light by the same means as all previous modes of illumination—that is, by the incandescence of unburned particles (carbon) of its own fuel. Most of these pleasantly glowing particles escaped from the flame still unburned and became unpleasant soot deposited on some other part of the environment (usually the ceiling). Welsbach's invention used the principle of the Bunsen burner to make combustion more complete, and the resultant hot flame produced incandescence of the mineral salts deposited on the mantle which capped the flame, giving a much whiter and cleaner light.

Neither gas lighting nor piped central heating at these early levels produced any serious architectural problems. Gas lighting fittings constituted the same sort of fire-risk as had candles, and large gasoliers had therefore to be hung well away from the walls, much as chandeliers had been, while the pipes to supply them were not bulky enough to call for much special provision of architectural spaces **[Plate 12]**. Hot water pipes were larger, but like gas pipes could be run under floors or above plaster ceilings, while the radiators usually found a natural and efficient place in the embrasures of windows, where they helped counter the chill down-draughts caused by air in contact with cold window-glass.

Air and its movements, however, were something of a puzzle to the Victorians who had little idea of the part played by relative humidity in provoking sensations of thermal and atmospheric discomfort. Obsessed by 'draughts' and 'vitiated air' and 'bad drains' they wasted money on patent ventilators that did not ventilate, and seized on the possibility of using the waste heat of gas lighting to convect away fouled air through ceiling grilles. These were used especially in public spaces such as theatres and schools where the massive 'Sunburner' lamps of the pre-Welsbach epoch could generate strong thermal currents with their naked gas flames (as many as fifty) **[Plate 11]**.

These 'illuminating furnaces' did need special chimneys above them, but otherwise put few demands on the architecture. Even more spectacular in this negative way was the small immediate effect of the parallel hygienic revolution which eventually disposed of the dreaded smell of 'bad drains'. In London, Edwin Chadwick's powerful advocacy of a properly water-borne sewage system, and its realization in the great programme of sewer-building by Sir Joseph Bazalgette in the sixties and early seventies transformed the hygienic infrastructure of the capital.

Water-borne sewage

In many of the richer houses of London, however, the flushing toilets essential to the success of this system already existed. The principle of flushing had been expounded by Sir Thomas Harrington as far back as the time of Elizabeth I, the mechanism was made practical by Joseph Bramah in 1778 **[Fig. 1]** and the modern water-trap (which locked away the worst of the smell) followed within the decade. While it had been illegal to flush these toilets into the primitive sewer system of London before Bazalgette's scheme was built, they did exist and had already found their place in better-off houses—usually directly above cess-pits under the cellars! When it became possible to connect them to the new sewers, the cess-pits could finally be abandoned, which was a considerable gain to public health since they were rarely emptied more than twice a year, and were often close to wells!

Figure 1 Joseph Bramah, flushing WC, 1788

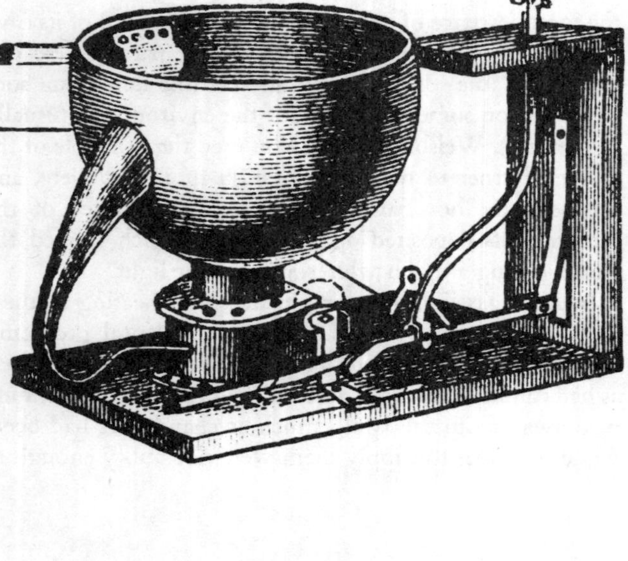

In institutional buildings, such as the London Board Schools erected after Forster's Education Act of 1870, toilet blocks continued to be built away from the main buildings even where they were connected to the sewers, and for good reason, it was a long time before the British ceased to regard toilets as a potential health-hazard. Yet this particular problem had been solved, effectively, a long way from their homes. Properly designed town sewerage systems leading to outfalls with even the most primitive treatment plant finally separated the foul effluents from the supplies of drinking water and eliminated the main cause of scourges such as cholera—the contamination of surface wells by seepages of untreated sewage.

Hot-air heating

In the meantime, however, the rise of hot-air heating was beginning to introduce unprecedented architectural problems. The traditional North European stove **[Plate 13]**, whether tiled or built from heavy cast-iron units, marked an advance on the Roman hypocaust because it delivered its heat directly into the volume of air to be warned, standing usually in the corner of the room but well out from the wall. The American lightweight Franklin stove **[Plate 14]**, built of thin iron plates, was a device of the same order, but of higher performance so that it often became red-hot in use. As a measure of safety and convenience therefore, ingenious builders in New England began, during the sixties, to locate their stoves out of the way in the basement, and conduct the hot air they generated through ducts to the various rooms, from a 'hot-box' round the top of the stove.

The problem here is that air, bulk for bulk, is an inefficient carrier of heat, compared with a medium like water, and a much greater volume of it must be moved around to achieve the same heating effect. While there is always the side-effect of improved ventilation to be set against the difficulties, the duct-work could often be of nine or twelve inches diameter, and that could rarely be accommodated in normal domestic constructions without special provisions.

In a single-storey building with a basement, these provisions were not too difficult to make, but where ducts

Figure 2 Elisha Graves Otis, safety elevator

had to be carried up through an inhabited storey (as to the bedrooms of a two-storey house) space for these risers was often hard to find. Occasionally a particular style of architecture would provide such spaces—classical modes with barrel-vaulted ceilings and apsidal ends to rooms often left usable triangular volumes above and behind the plaster-work, but simpler and more rectilinear styles often did not, and the difficulties encountered here were but early warning of some major architectural problems that were to emerge when engineers tried to take command of the internal atmosphere of larger constructions.

2 New building types

Many of the larger buildings where problems of environmental control were to be encountered were in themselves unprecedented in function and form. Office-blocks, the board schools, new types of hospitals, work-houses and prisons, were building types for which existed no customary forms and no immemorial rules of thumb for their successful design. The new problems they raised naturally invited the attentions of ingenious engineers, and their large bulk and high capital investment made it possible to think in terms of mechanical aids that were too large or too expensive to be used in domestic designs.

Lifts

The most notable of these aids was the passenger lift or elevator, increasingly used after Elisha Graves Otis had demonstrated his 'safety elevator' in 1854 [**Fig. 2**]. The combination of the elevator and the steel frame after 1870 is often credited with causing the 'rise of the skyscraper' but one can point to at least one power-driven device that is probably more consequential in this matter than the steel frame: the telephone [**Fig. 3**]. London's first exchange

Figure 3 An early telephone installation at Coleman Street, London, 1879

opened in 1879 and most central business districts had telephone systems before the eighties were out. And it is salutary to reflect that without the telephone the elevators of the new office blocks would have been permanently jammed with junior staff bearing written messages by hand! And it is even more salutary to try and imagine what these buildings would have been like without flushing toilets and main drainage!

Environmental control in multi-storey buildings

Even with these aids, however, many types of large buildings were showing signs of environmental and functional strain that only further architectural and technological ingenuity could remedy. Most of these problems were concerned with lighting and ventilation, for both of which windows continued to be the only effective sources. For this reason the board schools often had windows over twelve feet high standing on sills five feet above floor level, in order to gain maximum penetration of daylight across the depth of the room. Hospitals and other welfare buildings were usually built only one room thick, in order to ensure direct cross-ventilation the air being able to pass through windows on each side of a given ward. Office blocks were built around an open courtyard (usually around only three sides of it) in order to admit light and air to the back sides of all their limbs. Yet the limits of what natural light and air could achieve had already been reached by 1880, while appalled social reformers and medical men—Chadwick in England, Pettenkofer in Germany—demanded better standards still for those who had to use the buildings. The artificial lighting technology of the time could not hope to meet such standards; enough light by gas to combat the chronic eye strain of tailors and ledger clerks would have involved so much generation of heat that a ventilation crisis would have ensued.

More and bigger windows seemed for the moment to be the only way. The architects of the Chicago school, men like Louis Sullivan and John Wellborn Root (Units 7–8) spread their famous three-light Chicago windows until they might, by 1900, occupy as much as 45% of the external surface of the building. That gave better light; it might also have given better ventilation except that in many other cities as well as Chicago the atmosphere was so filthy that one opened a window at one's peril. Futhermore, there were environmental problems generated within the buildings themselves, such as the smells from heavily used toilet facilities, flushing though they might be. It soon became established good practice in planning buildings to isolate the toilets in some way: in Britain this led to the 'ventilated lobby' demanded in most of our building codes, in Chicago it lead to the grouping of the toilets along with the noisy elevators in a projection in the central lightwell at the back of the building—the Marquette block by Holabird and Roche, 1894, shows the most highly developed example of this type of plan (see Radiovision 29 booklet for radio programme 29) **[Plates 15–16]**.

In the end, only artificial ventilation could handle these problems. The necessary fan technology existed by 1860, and was being developed rapidly in such fields as forced-draught for steam ships—neither the furnaces of the boilers, nor the remoter habitable spaces of the ships themselves, could be adequately served by normal convection currents of air, though such thermal or 'gravity' ventilation could be used in land-borne structures where room could be found for large volumes of very slow-moving air. To achieve such thermal movement the Liverpool doctor and hygienist, John Hayward, combined a stack of lobbies, connected by grilles in floors and ceilings, into a gigantic vertical duct in his 'draught-free' house of 1867 **[Plate 17]**. In Cuthbert Brodrick's town hall for Leeds **[Plates 17–19]** designed the following year, twelve-foot-square ducts for thermal ventilation of the public spaces rose so far above the cornice line that they compete for attention with the dome and other more conventional features of classical architecture.

Electricity

Both the bulk and the unreliability of these natural methods made fan-impelled ventilation ever more attractive. The power sources were already to hand in the form of steam engines and, after 1876, the tireless slow-turning Otto engine running on town gas. By the end of the eighties electricity was to join the list of power sources, but its real contribution to the heat and ventilation problem lay in the fact that, as a lighting medium, it generated vastly less heat than all previous fuels (see Part One, Section 3). But if fan ventilation was more efficient, it still could not be shrunk below certain minimum sizes given the technology of the time, and was thus only available for large structures. There however, it began not only to impose weighty demands on structure and space, but also to create opportunities which cunning architects could seize for adventures in space and structure that had not been possible before.

The Glasgow School of Art

The first building in which environmental machinery can be seen in this way as a direct contributor to the rise of modern architecture is probably the School of Art in Glasgow, 1898–1909, by Charles Rennie Mackintosh **[Plates 20–22** and Units 3–4]. This may sound paradoxical because Mackintosh is generally discussed in the literature as an Arts and Crafts designer, rather than a Machine Aesthete, but he was not alone in his generation in being able to make effective use of mechanical and electrical services without feeling required to make a big scene about it.

The ventilation system of the school was a 'Plenum' in

which, following the method devised by William Key of Glasgow in the eighties, the fan was used to fill the building with warmed (or cool) air under slight pressure. (See Broadcasting Supplement to television programme 22). Thus in the winter, when life could have been very hard on nude models posing in the huge north-lit studios of the school, warmed air would be seeping out of the building at points where, otherwise, cold air might have been leaking in.

The Plenum system worked by forcing hot air from a central plant around a closed building. What do you think might have been the major advantages and disadvantages of this system?

● The main advantages of the Plenum system were that it required no hot-water pipes or radiators, caused no draughts and allowed fine adjustment of the air temperature. Its main disadvantages were that it has to work in a sealed system (open windows destroyed its working principle) and that because it involved sophisticated mechanical and electrical plant it required skilled maintenance and administration. ●

The duct work to distribute this air can be seen on Mackintosh's original plans and was an integral part of his design, aesthetically as well as environmentally. Much of it still survives as part of the visible furnishings of the studios and other main work spaces, but in the nineteen-thirties it fell out of use (apparently through inadequate maintenance) and was replaced by conventional hot-water radiators throughout the building (previously they had been used only at strategic points under large areas of glass). Immediately it became clear—and still is—how closely Mackintosh's spatial effects were related to his mechanical aids, and the results for the carefully composed interior of his famous library were subtly disastrous. Among all its built-in bookshelves and cupboards there was literally nowhere to install the radiators except on the step at the entrance to each of the oriel window-bays. The radiators now make an effective fence against entry into the bays, thus destroying their functions as places to consult works of art by natural daylight, while the carefully modulated flow of space between the galleried and rather dark library and the pools of light under the windows is visually broken, thus destroying Mackintosh's aesthetic intentions. ●

Read Appendix II (from *The Architecture of the Well-tempered Environment*) and using the descriptions and drawings reproduced in Figs. 4 and 5, trace the movement of air from the point where it enters the building to the point where it leaves. How far is it true to say that design of either the Royal Victoria Hospital or the Larkin Building is dictated by the ventilating system?

Figure 4 Frank Lloyd Wright, the Larkin Building, Buffalo, N.Y., 1906, isometric section

1. Fresh air intake
2. Tempered air distribution
3. Foul air and exhaust
4. Utilities duct
5. Tempered air outlet grilles under edge of balconies

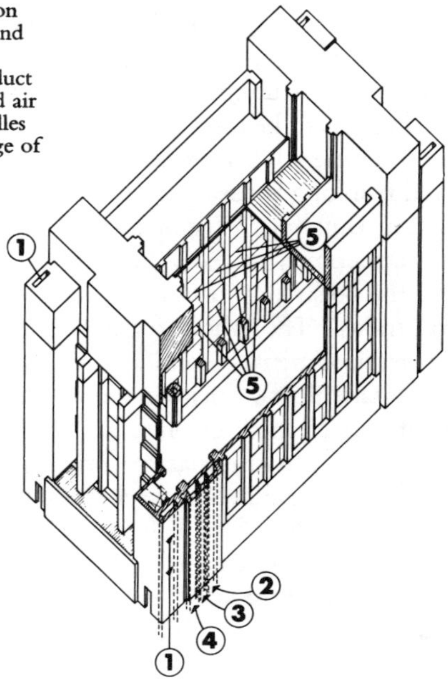

Figure 5 Henman and Cooper, the Royal Victoria Hospital, Belfast, 1903, isometric section

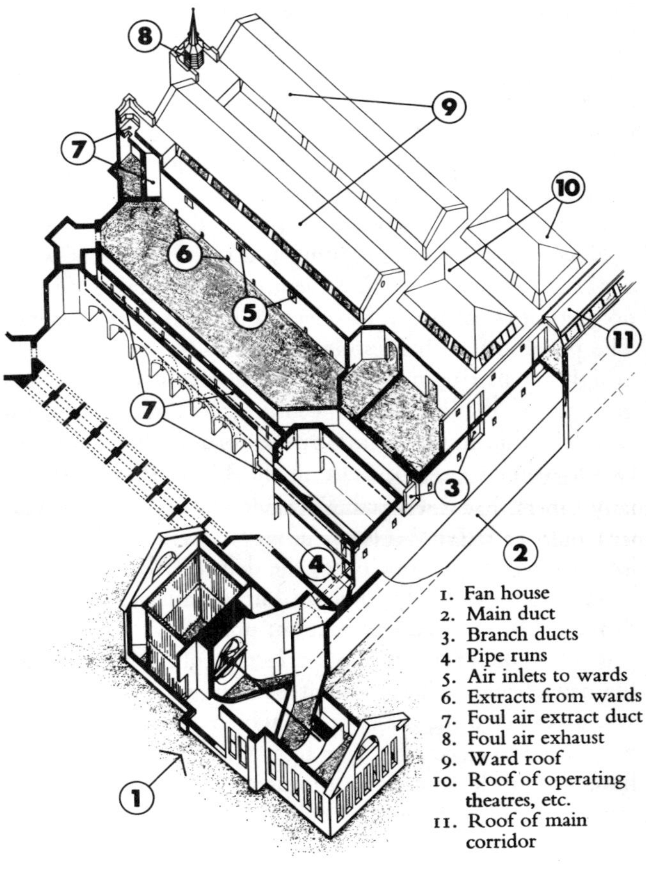

1. Fan house
2. Main duct
3. Branch ducts
4. Pipe runs
5. Air inlets to wards
6. Extracts from wards
7. Foul air extract duct
8. Foul air exhaust
9. Ward roof
10. Roof of operating theatres, etc.
11. Roof of main corridor

• In Henman and Cooper's Royal Victoria Hospital the form of the building is dictated by the demands of the Plenum system: a single structural volume is used so that hot-air trunking does not have to pass from one building to another (thereby losing expensive heat) and the rectilinear compactness of the plan was designed to follow the paths of the hot-air trunking. (In the Plenum system straight trunking was to be used wherever possible because there can be an efficiency loss of up to 40% caused by air drag if curved trunking is used.)

Of the Larkin Building, Wright himself acknowledged that it was 'hermetically sealed . . . to keep the interior space clear of the poisonous gases in the smoke from New York central trains'. The whole form of the building is dictated by environmental considerations. The corner towers act as intake ducts, drawing the air into the basement where it was cleaned and heated; the air was then blown up riser ducts in the massive brick panels visible in the exterior and distributed on each floor through outlets under the balustrades of the balconies. The same brick panels are also used as exhaust ducts. Because the windows have no functional purpose they were set high under the ceilings of each tier, above the filing cabinets. •

3 Electricity and lighting

Like most of his generation who had access to it, Mackintosh also tried to exploit the new possibilities of electric lighting. His experiments were not radical however, and were largely confined to devising light fittings which, however handsome, are only light fittings, and are disposed in a relatively conventional way about the room. He was not one of the great innovators in this field, which had, in any case, just passed out of its first phase of wild invention and experiment at that time.

Nevertheless, electric lighting was still a source of wonder and enthusiasm, an invention comparable to the domestication of fire in its effect on human environments. The possibility of harnessing electricity for purposes such as lighting had been discussed speculatively since the beginning of the nineteenth century. Technically it was almost within human grasp by the forties when inventors like Swann in Britain, Starr in the USA [**Plate 24**] and many others, had devised workable ancestors of the filament bulb of today. None, however, was workable for long enough to be much use; the delicate filaments either broke or, more likely, quickly burned away in the residual air left by imperfect vacuum pumps.

Pending the production of perfect vacuums in which the filaments could be incandescent without burning, attention was diverted to the arc lamp, in which a spark was struck between two electrodes. The light was brilliant and could function in the normal atmosphere, but the electrodes burned away and needed constant adjustment and the equipment was noisy and dangerous (**Plate 25** shows a Jabocklov arc lamp). Difficult to domesticate, it functioned best in the open or in large spaces where a few powerful arc-lamps could be hung high enough to be out of harm's way. Their power was sensational by comparison with any other form of lighting and their appearance in public places and in international electrical exhibitions (Paris 1881, Frankfurt 1891) helped to dramatize the promise of electric light.

But that promise could only be realized when the light could be domesticated, and for this a series of technical breakthroughs were needed. None of these was fortuitous; each had long been identified and was ultimately achieved by laborious development work. One was a practicable dynamo technology, achieved through the work of engineers like Gramme and Siemens by the end of the eighties. By this means, large and continuous power supplies could be achieved on demand through relatively compact engine/generator sets, rather than through vast assemblies of chemical batteries. In the same decade, the availability of the Sprengle pump made 'hard' vacuums possible and the problem of filaments burning away could be overcome. Just before 1880 both Swann and (in the US) Edison arrived simultaneously at commercially viable lamp-bulbs, using filaments derived ultimately from cotton thread or paper strips.

The most crucial step required, however, was to devise a safe and reliable system of switching, distributing and metering the current between generator and bulb. This was the true triumph of Thomas Alva Edison [**Plate 28**] backed by his long experience in telegraphy and the remarkable boldness of the businessmen who put up the capital for the intensive development work required. In London S. Z. Ferranti arrived, a little later and by more idiosyncratic methods, at an equally workable distribution system, while in the early eighties George Westinghouse's hydro-electric plant at Niagara initiated the long-distance distribution of high-voltage alternating current.

At the beginning of the eighties, electricity from the mains was available in down-town New York, around Holborn Viaduct in London, thanks to Edison, in Mayfair (Ferranti) a little later and also Kensington (Crompton), [**Plates 26–27**]. From these concentrated and highly profitable central areas, mains electricity spread by the beginning of the nineties to richer inner-ring suburbs, where conversion of existing houses to electric lighting was a thrilling business by the middle of the decade. By 1900 electricity was into the outer suburbs, where it was already a normal first installation in newly-built houses being constructed for buyers to whom the suburbs were being made accessible by fast electric railways.

It was in these new suburbs that electricity can be seen making its most revolutionary contributions to new concepts of domestic design, for these were the areas where architects like Mackintosh, Wright, Voysey, Behrens and others of the pioneer generation did most of their work. Art Nouveau, *Jugendstil*, Arts and Crafts, the California Bungalow style all bear witness to the liberating effect of electric light. That liberation depended almost entirely from a single factor—that electricity gave light without flame.

The importance of this fact was noted by even the earliest commentators on electric light—see John Slater's comments in Appendix 3. Even though the ordinary filament bulb wastes much of the power it burns in producing heat rather than light, it still produces far less heat than any conceivable gas installation of equivalent candlepower. Furthermore, the absence of combustion means that it needs no oxygen supply, and produces no waste gases or soot—it can thus operate in places (e.g. under water) where other illuminants would be unthinkable. And it constitutes only the slightest fire-risk. Light, bright, subtle and delicate interiors in accordance with the developing taste of the period were practicable almost before the taste had crystallized. The new light could be concentrated and of high intensity as bulbs became more powerful year by year, or it could be distributed in small sources for even lighting of low intensity—and a room could be changed from the one to the other at the touch of a switch. The lamps could be concealed above coves and cornices, behind glass or grilles, integrated into elaborate carpentry, could be shaded with delicate silks or semi-precious stones. So much was possible, and so much was done with such artistic effect, that one may wonder if the almost deliberately bald and crude lighting practised in the twenties by architects of the avant-garde was not a reaction against a surfeit of the electric lit interiors in which they grew up.

Not all the pioneers had the taste or the ability to elaborate such imaginative schemes of course. Neither Mackintosh, Voysey nor Behrens were in the front rank of innovation. Behrens's work is usually remarkably uninspired for the man who was director of design to the mightly Allgemeine Elektrizitäts Gesellschaft, and not to be compared to his brilliant contemporary J. M. Olbrich whose Gluckert House in Darmstadt (see Units 5–6, Plate 10) used pinpoint patterns of exposed low-power bulbs to create new spatial effects in otherwise unremarkable spaces.

Wright's Robie house

None of the Europeans, however brilliant, could manage to equal Frank Lloyd Wright in the use of electric lighting. Wright, it must be allowed, enjoyed the advantage of a less hide-bound architectural culture and clients who expected performance for their money, and out of the two there emerged a kind of 'total system approach' to the domestic environment that is without parallel. For instance, in the Robie House (**Plates 29–30**, Unit 7–8, Plates 49–50), his masterpiece and not quite completed when he had to leave Chicago in 1909, deep roof overhangs shelter the large areas of glass against the noonday and afternoon sun, while a deeply shaded entrance court on the north side combines with an equally shaded ground-floor to form a 'cool air tank' which tempers the whole house in summer. The main living-room on the first floor [**Plate 29**] is glazed for nearly three-quarters of its perimeter, and since practically every window can be opened, natural ventilation can take advantage of the lightest breeze from whatever quarter. In spite of the large amount of glass, the room is not over-chilled in winter (or not as Wright designed it) for heat was to be provided at the rate of a radiator to every window, and where these windows were French doors opening down to the floor, the radiators were to be concealed under brass grilles behind the threshold, so that a curtain of warmed air was to ascend right round the room.

The electric lighting for the long and handsome space comes from visible glass gloves carried in wooden *japonaiserie* brackets along the edge of the upstand in the centre of the ceiling.

But concealed lights also contributed; they were set above wooden grilles let into the lower parts of the ceiling down each side of the room, and controlled by theatrical dimmers so that the amount of background lighting could be varied. By a typically ingenious piece of design, the heat of these concealed lights pulls a gentle flow of spent air out of the room and up into the main roof-space which it helps to air in damp winter weather. Finally, this air is extracted through a thermal duct built into the side of the main chimney which provides its heat. A neat pattern of gaps in the brickwork on the side of the chimney marks the point where this well-used air is finally exhausted to the outside atmosphere.

European architects

The reasons why few European architects ever rivalled Wright in the management of mechanical and electrical services go beyond the dimensions of genius. They are climatic, technical and economic, and so closely intertwined that they must almost be seen as cultural differences. Wright in the Middle West was designing for variations of heat, cold and humidity that could not be paralleled in Europe. He was working in an economy that was technically advanced, and preferred to spend money on running costs rather than on prime investments, because fuel was cheap and building materials often expensive. Wright, like most builders in the Middle West, had a natural tendency to put up relatively flimsy lightweight structures, whether in wood or steel, and make up their environmental deficiencies with energy-consuming equipment, as had been the American way ever since the introduction of the fast-heating Franklin stove.

In Europe—as in the Latin parts of the Americas—it remained however, the custom to work with heavy, heat-conserving, heat-insulating structures, into which mechanical aids (ruinously expensive on fuel, compared to American costs) were admitted grudgingly, almost as admissions of failure. Many architects then (and still today) seemed to regard them as mere fancy novelties that ought not to be allowed to affect the architectural conception in plan, section or construction. Wright, contrariwise, was working in a culture that set great store by invention and expected to see all inventions put to work as soon as practicable however marginal or radical their expected effects.

The rate of invention triggered by electric lighting was so high, however, that its effects tended to be radical everywhere, and the outstanding inventions deserve to be chronicled because of their almost convulsive effect on domestic (and other) life. The power and efficiency of filament bulbs escalated annually until the end of the twenties. Edison had patented the basic principles of the fluorescent lamp before 1900, though it took forty years to put a viable model on the market. In the meantime, gas-discharge tubes ('neon tubes' in common parlance) were in use on the façade of a London cinemas as early as 1913 [**Plate 31**].

Domestic electric appliances

Once a lighting circuit had brought mains electricity into the house, it could be used to power appliances to perform household tasks that were laborious to perform by hand, or dangerous or difficult to power by other fuels. All over the world the electric flat-iron followed lighting into even poor houses almost as soon as the wiring was installed. It was followed at varying intervals by a series of other appliances which are in common use today and were, for the most part, invented and even marketed before 1910. The list includes the electric kettle, cooker, immersion heater, electric blanket, vacuum cleaner—though the domestic electric refrigerator was not available, even in the US until after World War I.

Nearly all these devices were European inventions, but underwent their crucial development to domestic levels of utility in the US. Thus, the fractional horsepower AC motor, essential to many items of equipment, was invented in Hungary by Nikola Tesla, but developed and manufactured by Westinghouse in whose AC 'empire' it had a natural and profitable role to play. The architectural results of this development, one may note in passing, were negative in one instance. Tesla's motor could be made small enough to be pushed around the floor on the end of a broom handle; as a result the vacuum cleaner could be a piece of portable equipment, instead of a permanent installation with vacuum tubes running through the walls to suck dust from extension nozzles into a central container in the basement (see Broadcasting Supplement to television programme 22). One or two such installations were made in the US before the First War, but the portable appliance type of solution prevailed, for obvious reasons.

In this rise of the 'Appliance Culture' traditional differences between the two sides of the Atlantic become very clear. US enthusiasm and commercialism rapidly bred a 'cult of comfort', and an ethic of mechanical consumption freed from traditional restrains of thrift, attitudes of which electrical equipment in the home has become symbolic. In Europe, by contrast, these were seen as matters of architectural and philosophical concern; the appliances were part of the 'Problem of the Machine', and their successful incorporation into the canons of architecture tended to be seen as an intellectual breakthrough of cultural importance. In *Form and Function* No. 92, you will find Marcel Breuer talking about the problem of 'civilizing the machine', an exercise that most Americans would have regarded as pointless or fruitless.

Thus, while there flourished in Europe of the twenties the 'Machine Aesthetic', it is difficult to find anything equivalent in North America. As a result European architects continued to regard the Americans as architecturally backward—yet it is clear from cases of European architects who worked in America in the twenties and thirties, men like Rudolph Schindler or Richard Neutra, that in the more relaxed atmosphere of the States they could be both technically *and* aesthetically more adventurous than in Europe.

Eric Mendelsohn

Almost the only architect in Europe who could handle mechanical and electrical services with the same fluency as Wright was Eric Mendelsohn. In a series of shops designed in the twenties he developed the expressive use of lighting, particularly concealed lighting, and this phase of his architecture achieved its masterpiece in the Universum Cinema, Berlin, 1928, in which all environmental aids are blended into a unified composition which Mendelsohn celebrated in a kind of poem (Appendix 4).

The other great Europeans of that time, men like Gropius and Le Corbusier, seem curiously constrained by contrast: their heating and lighting installations seem conventional and uninventive, their impact on the viewer deriving from their visually aggressive disposition and their often uncomfortable environmental effects. Until the end of the twenties, Le Corbusier was prepared to use naked lamp-bulbs of high power in full view in the centre of visually unmodulated ceilings. It was clear that for Europeans, mechanical and electrical services were seen less as physical comforts than a 'phenomenon of spiritual discipline', in van Doesburg's words. Perhaps the finest and most telling monument to this unrelaxed European approach is to be found not in the work of any of the great and famous masters of the International Style but in the Dalsace House,

Paris, 1928–33, by Pierre Chareau and the Dutch architect Bernard Bijvoet. Known as the *Maison de Verre* because its exterior is almost entirely glass brick, its interior combines machine-age materials, and concealed heating and lighting with elaborately 'machiniste' ingenuity. Almost alone of the great Modern houses of its time, however, it delivers mechanical performance in fact as well as symbol (see Radiovision booklet for radio programme 15).

Using the texts and appendices and illustrations in this unit, and any others that seem relevant among your course material, itemize the differences between the interior environments of houses by Frank Lloyd Wright on the one hand, and Le Corbusier on the other, going into every detail your sources permit. Which architect's approach seems to you to provide a more comfortable and satisfying living space?

● Obviously, there is no one answer to a question of this sort—it is a matter of personal taste. In such a subjective area critical and historical criteria cannot operate. It would be a good idea, however, to bear in mind the fundamental differences between the houses you have chosen: for instance, climate, site, client, budget, materials and date. ●

Part two The fully conditioned interior

1 Le Corbusier's experiments

As the reference to Mendelsohn's cinema may suggest, this primarily domestic narrative of the rise of electricity has overrun some important developments in the servicing of larger buildings. Throughout the twenties architects and engineers can be seen working almost independently towards concepts of the interior of a building as a totally controlled, totally artificial environment of some sort. Their understandings and their motivations in this ambition were, understandably, quite different, even when they finally coincided in a building such as the UN Secretariat.

In that progress towards the Secretariat tower, Le Corbusier had started from a passion for all-glass walls, and the rationalizations he had offered in their justification. Given a framed construction in concrete, he had argued in 1926, the walls as such no longer carry weight. Much lighter non-structural materials can be substituted on the exterior, and those in the interior can be located at will or according to functional need, rather than where the loads fall. These interior arrangements he called *le plan libre* and they are fixedly associated in his mind and projects with his ideal solution to he lightweight exterior wall, *le pan de verre*. This all-glass wall is not only the lightest reliable barrier against external weather, it also admits health-giving sunlight to the interior, while permitting maximum views outwards—his writings abound in sketches extolling these qualities.[1]

Unfortunately, as he soon discovered, single-thickness glass is a poor thermal insulator, and suffers other deficiencies besides: it offers no visual privacy and very little acoustic privacy either; it has dubious fireproofing qualities and runs with condensation in cold weather. Over the years these deficiencies have been made good by Le Corbusier and his followers and imitators by a slow and additive process, adding a fresh layer to the composite wall to deal with each deficiency, beginning with the *brise-soleil* on the outside and finishing with the air-conditioners on the back of the upstand fireproof wall on the inside—an ensemble considerably thicker in the end than the masonry wall it sought to replace!

Le Corbusier's own interest in these necessary compensatory devices was awakened—forcibly—by two large projects that came his way in the late twenties. Centrosoyus (see Units 13–14) in Moscow, 1928–33, and the Cité de Refuge, Paris, 1930–2. Both were very big institutional buildings of slab form for which he ordained total glazing on the main façades. The consequences were to be difficult enough in Paris, and promised to be disastrous in the climate of Moscow. His proposed solution to the problems of both buildings was two-fold: firstly *la respiration exacte* (freely translated: exact air) and secondly *le mur neutralisant* (neutralizing wall). The former was artificial ventilation, the latter was an insulating wall, but neither, separately or in conjunction, was as simple as that. They combine into a ruthlessly logical, uneconomic, complicated and almost totally impractical environmental control system.

This system calls for a building with two separate and sealed air-circulation routes. One, internally, provides ventilation on a closed circuit, passing used air back through cleansing and re-oxygenating devices (as in a submarine or space-ship) and returning it to the habitable spaces. The other system passes warmed or cooled air between the two layers of glass of the neutralizing wall, thus insulating the building from heat or cold outside. All this according to Le Corbusier (and according to nobody else; even his favourite mechanical and electrical services consultant Gustave Lyon was guarded about it) could be so effectively done that the internally circulating air of the *respiration exacte* would always remain at 18°C without itself being heated or cooled.

Neither building was, in fact, built according to this system. The Cité de Refuge had a sealed single-glazed façade and a hot-air heating system which worked notably well in the winter. No cooling was provided for summer, however, and in the end opening windows had to be installed, and a *brise-soleil* added after World War II. Centrosoyus was built with conventional hot-water radiators and even there the idea of a sealed façade was scouted by his Russian clients on the ground that Soviet air was so much cleaner than capitalist air that it need not be kept out of the building!

Even in less ideological or poverty-stricken circumstances, it is doubtful if anyone would seriously have let Le Corbusier put his system into effect. It was a beautiful intellectual construction but Gustave Lyon could rapidly have demonstrated to him its impracticalities and extravagances. Yet so great was his prestige, and so anxious was the Saint-Gobain company to sell more glass, that scientific tests were run in a specially designed experimental chamber. The published results were inconclusive and the scheme was not pursued commercially.

At almost exactly the same time, something similar was in fact built in the US, (a bank building in New York), but here the internal air was drawn between double glazed walls—an impure solution that might not have appealed to Le Corbusier's 'logic'—and returned to the interior. However, even this system was not repeated. The pragmatical engineers of the US had simpler and more edonomical solutions to hand.

2 The development of air-conditioning

American practice had, indeed, already arrived at technologies which could be combined to deliver all the performance that an architect like Le Corbusier could ask for, while additionally coping with problems like humidity

[1] In some of Le Corbusier's buildings, however, the *pan-de-verre* was made of *opaque* glass bricks.

which he had not faced, and with far higher degrees of 'fail-safe' than his totally sealed circulations. By the time he visited the US in 1934, Le Corbusier could have visited many such systems installed, and certainly did experience one, in Radio City, by which he was greatly impressed. Indeed he reported that air-conditioning was 'everywhere', in that *pays aux voltages puissants* (high-voltage country).

He may have been mistaken, even so, for many of the places he seems to have believed to be air-conditioned were, in fact, only ventilated, a distinction that is not always understood. The distinction had, however, been clearly formulated by the fathers of air-conditioning even before such a service could be delivered. The inventor of the term 'air-conditioning' (the engineer Stuart Cramer) had defined it thus in a patent application of 1906: 'to include humidifying, air-cleaning, heating and ventilation'. The powered supply of cleaned and heated air had been possible since the 1860s.

The fundamental innovation of the air-conditioners was the control of humidity, something beyond human ingenuity before that time. Cramer had perceived the basic method for this—cooling the air until excess moisture condensed out as dew—but it was Willis Carrier who, in one of the most brilliant recorded flashes of technological inspiration in this century, perceived that the most effective way of doing it was the paradoxical one of spraying water into the air-stream!

It is interesting to note that Samuel Cleland Davidson's installation at the Royal Victoria Hospital, Belfast (see Appendix 2) had effectively achieved air-conditioning by a very similar method, and the hospital can therefore claim to have been the first building in the world to be air-conditioned for human comfort. Davidson's main commercial and inventive interests, however, lay in other directions and he may not have fully appreciated what he had achieved. The matter was not pursued, and the centre of air-conditioning technology in Britain moved to Glasgow as a natural succession to William Key's work on the Plenum system of ventilation. This Scottish activity, however, never rivalled the inventiveness of the American engineers led and dominated by Willis Havilland Carrier, and it came nowhere near it in total bulk.

Cinemas

In the first instance it was the needs of environmentally sensitive industrial processes that forced these US development forward, and if human beings became more comfortable it was only as a by-product of their service as workers in these processes. The characteristic type of 'comfort job' (in Carrier's inelegant phrase) that emerged in the twenties was the theatre or cinema installation (see Broadcasting Supplements, television programme 22). In these, cooled, dried and filtered air was allowed to settle slowly over the audience from diffusers in the ceiling, in a soothing blanket, after which it was withdrawn through ducts under the floor, reconditioned, mixed with fresh air and returned to the auditorium. **Plate 32** shows the Plenum chamber in the Astoria Cinema, Finsbury Park, and **Plate 33** shows some of the architectural effects made possible in cinemas, exemplified by W. E. Trent's New Victoria.

These comfort-jobs were only commercially practicable because they were close to being industrial. Profits were measurable and the value of air-conditioning, which was expensive and bulky, could be directly shown. More important, the big single-volume, single-function auditorium was much like a factory-space in its environmental characteristics and requirements. Where a building was subdivided into many smaller spaces having differing requirements and characteristics, the problem was much harder to handle. Thus, while most of the Grand Hotels around the world were air-conditioning their dining rooms and other large public spaces by the end of the twenties, no attempt was made to condition individual bedrooms—the ductwork would have been ruinously expensive and too bulky to be accommodated without major structural alterations.

Offices

Although Carrier had some successes in reworking his traditional type of central-plan conditioning systems to office building requirements, as in the ingenious and pioneering Philadelphia Saving Fund Society building of 1932 (see Radiovision booklet, pp. 102–103, Figs. 11–17), (architects, Howe and Lescaze), he only fully resolved the problem with his Weathermaster system of 1937 [**Plate 34**] which has become the norm for all finely subdivided systems ever since. Humidity-controlled air is distributed at high velocity through small-bore ducts, which are much easier to accommodate in most kinds of architecture. It enters the rooms through mixer units under the windows, where it is heated or cooled by being passed over pipes through which hot or cold water flows. More importantly, the velocity of the air is reduced by mixing it with a far larger quantity of recirculated air from the room itself, so that instead of emerging with a deafening 'jet-roar' it rises gently as a blanket over the face of the window glass—and at a temperature which can be regulated by the occupants of the room. The result is an extremely sensitive and sophisticated system of environmental control which can respond to small-scale changes of need—but it still has to rely on some extremely massive plant somewhere in the building. Thus, in the UN Secretariat, the installations in the rooms are so unobtrusive that they pass almost unnoticed, which is quite an achievement in a building that has little wasted room in which to conceal anything at all. But if one looks at the exterior one can see that at least four full floors are given over to mechanical and electrical plant, and there are two more in the basements! **[Plate 1]**.

Can you think of one more invention which was to complete the story of full environmental control? What were its consequences?

● The invention was the fluorescent light tube which became available at the end of the thirties. This cool, low power light source reduced the total load of heat that used to be swept away. Armed with these it was possible to think seriously about building office blocks with deep, artificially-lit plans, without the usual re-entrants for light and air at the back. Without the fluorescent tube the rectangular slab plan of the UN Secretariat would have been unthinkable, except at incredible expense.

The other invention, which lies slightly outside the ostensible period covered by this unit but demands inclusion for the sake of completeness and because of its sensational implications, was the packaged domestic air-conditioner. Unthinkable before 1939, it was made possible by wartime advances in the miniaturization of refrigeration equipment. A novelty in 1951, its manufacture was a major industry in 1955 **[Plate 35]**. Sophisticated internally, it needed skill neither for its installation nor operation—it was simply a matter of 'Plug In, Switch On,' and air-conditioning passed for ever beyond the control of either architects or mechanical and electrical services consultants. ●

3 The totally controlled interior

Is there a building type which really epitomizes and makes explicit all these environmental innovations in the period under study and the reactions of architects to them? There is such a type, the radio-centre, and there is really one single building that epitomizes the type not only as architecture but as a social phenomenon as well, Broadcasting House, London, 1932 **[Plates 36** and **38–45]**. The social phenomenon most obviously in question is the scattering effect of the new media of communications. The movie palaces that housed the first comfort-jobs may have been sophisticated exercises of mechanical and electrical ingenuity, but they still brought audiences together in concentrated masses as had the theatres of earlier days. Yet given the 'wireless' the environment of a symphony concert could be a lonely Scottish croft or the deck-house of a trawler in the North Sea. Conversely the environment of a bed-sitter in Pimlico could be transformed, in part, into that of Plymouth Sound by the addition of sound-effects of creaking ropes, shivering timbers and the mewling of those notorious seagulls.

This particular industrial revolution in the human environment did not find its true prophet until Marshall McLuhan, but its first and most impressive monuments are of the same generation as Centrosoyus or The Philadelphia Savings Fund building. Even so, there must appear a paradox in the creation of anything so solid and so local as a monument to anything so ethereal and distributed as radio. The paradox depends on a peculiar circumstance—that radio be seen as a centralized national service under government control, rather than as a localized, distributed service under commercial control as in the USA (Radio City in New York does not really break this rule; it was the result of a financial freak).

The centralized view might be covertly political, as in Germany, where three independent companies combined to build the Rundfunkhaus, Berlin, 1930 **[Plate 37]** without waiting for Nazi instructions to do so, or might be quite explicit, as in Britain, where John Reith's interpretation of the lessons of the General Strike combined with his own moral elitism to produce a service reliably, though not by legal obligation, at the disposal of Westminster, centralized and permanently in the grip of what was described as 'a siege mentality'.

The actual building of Broadcasting House (architect Val Myer), expressed both aspects of the BBC's corporate mentality. As far as centralization was concerned the facts were manifest: the building contained, when first in full operation, nearly seventy per cent of all the studio space in the country, and an even larger proportion of the corporation's office space. The siege aspects were also manifest and were commented on by the architect Howard Robertson, who observed that the staff could live, eat, sleep and 'produce music, plays and noises-to-taste' even though the public 'might invade the corridors and even the offices'.

The apparently defensive format, however, has purely technical justifications which bulked considerably larger than the need for defence in times of civil strife. The building is planned in three concentric layers. The outer ring consists of offices and other rooms which require only normal environmental aids, natural lighting and ventilation. The next layer inwards is made up of the famous corridors on which all internal circulation depends, and which also serve to help insulate the third layer, the central core of studios and technical services.

This central location of all radio work-spaces was required by the nature of the work and the perfectionist mystique of the BBC's powerful cadre of engineers, then headed by Norman Ashridge. While the engineers felt that the sound to be transmitted was safe enough once it was entrusted to their wiring and equipment, they knew not what impurities might enter the channel in the perilous passage of air between mouth (or musical instrument) and microphone. To this end they ensured that no foreign sound could enter the studios, so successfully that the silence in Broadcasting House studios is more intense than that in any other studios in the world.

To achieve this the central core of the building has a separate structure of load-bearing brick so that it cannot pick up vibration from the concrete-framed outer parts of the building, all approaches and anterooms are carpeted, and all studios are approached via 'sound-locks' with at least two heavy doors between studio and corridor. There is no normal air-borne communication with any space outside the studio, not even the adjoining control room. Other than in situations where the existing microphones can be used, communication has to be visual—by hand signals through the double glazing of the control room window, or by means of coloured lights.

Yet subservience to the demands of technological perfectionism goes further than this. No airborne sound can enter the studio because no normal air enters the studio—the studios would be uninhabitable if they were not artificially ventilated, and this requirement made Broadcasting House, for a full decade after its completion in 1932, the most elaborately air-conditioned building in Britain. But even the most advanced air-conditioning experts in the world could not satisfy the technical fanatics of the BBC, and the 'commercial silence' offered by Carriers fell below their standards on two counts—the plant did actually generate noise which might find its way down the ducts to the studios, and the ducts might also transmit sound from one studio to another [**Plates 39–43**].

To counter the first, the cross-section of the ducts was expanded so that air could flow around sound absorbing panels without too much reduction of velocity, and to counter the second the plant was divided into four separate units, each of which fed studios as far apart as possible, and this attenuation of sound by distance was increased by lengthening the ducts by ingenious foldings back in the thickness of the walls. This may not have been the most sophisticated air-conditioning installation of its time, but it was certainly one of the most complex, and taken together with the extensive system of lights for illumination and communication in the studio block, the other elaborate networks for communication and control, and the electronics required for the actual business of broadcasting, made this a building more completely at the mercy of mechanical and electrical services than any other of its generation.

How could architects and designers respond to such a situation? Val Myer's main envelope has always been dismissed as undistinguished—a Portland stone battleship with Georgian windows and a little sculpture (by Eric Gill) and only the three transmitter masts on to the roof to reveal its true functions. In the entrance hall, with its famous Latin (!) inscription, this blend of Art Deco and gutless classicism continues and it is only in the corridors and beyond that the design comes to life. There are a number of easily identifiable reasons for this. The most obvious is that the Studio Decoration Committee under V. H. Goldsmith set itself a deliberately functionalist programme, citing 'Fitness for Purpose' as its watchword. More decisive, however, was their decision to entrust the work to a team of younger, avant-garde (to various degrees) designers, headed by Raymond McGrath. And further, there was a real job for the studio decorator to do since

> the studio was a dungeon before decoration . . . the tall artificial window which has been introduced gives airiness and banishes any feeling of confinement. . . .

(to quote a report in the *Architectural Review*, 1932)

Such environmental fakery could be a valid task even for a committed functionalist, since many of those who would be called upon to speak or perform in the studios would be unused to such totally artificial environments, and might well react badly to them. With almost everything else fixed by the fanaticism for perfect sound, the visual was almost the only aspect open to manipulation for atmosphere. Even so, only one of the studios was done in any kind of period style—a sort of VIP study, complete with a chair once used by Arnold Bennett, by Dorothy Warren Trotter [**Plate 44**]. Edward Maufe's religious broadcast studio was—as might be expected for so solemn a subject—somewhat in the pompous style of the exterior, but much modified by acoustic requirements (and because Maufe, later to become the architect of Guildford Cathedral, was a better architect than Myer) [**Plate 45**]. But McGrath's own dance-band studio BB was an entirely different matter, blending acoustic materials and strong colours in an uninhibited streamline-moderne composition.

Even more stiking are the more 'technical' studios for news, drama and special effects, etc., by Wells Coates and Serge Chermayeff (see Unit 19). Here the interior designs had to incorporate technical equipment such as gramophone turntables and control consoles. There were no good architectural precedents for the design of this kind of space, but both designers were keen adepts of the Machine Aesthetic from the continent and probably believed (with the *Architectural Review*) that 'the (BBC) engineers are artists in themselves. The neatness and efficiency of the machinery . . . is its beauty.' Thus they worked hard to adapt the idiom of the International Style to the engineer's aesthetic of the electronic equipment they had to house and produced some of the liveliest interior designs of their day anywhere in the world. Wells Coates's drama-effects studio control desk, most notably, so far transcends the usual kind of English copying of continental models that it bursts right out of its period and looks more like something designed for the Festival of Britain more than twenty years later.

Yet such designs were in many ways the chance by-products of freak conditions. It so happened that the rise of this kind of advanced, electrically based technology coincided in Britain with the idea of the state-instituted public corporation as a way of containing new innovations of which the ruling classes were half afraid. The BBC was a way of containing a politically explosive form of mass communication; London Transport was another such public corporation. The heads of both, John Reith and Frank Pick, saw themselves as some new kind of institutional Medici, called upon to patronize the arts and raise the standards of public taste. Under only marginally different circumstances these corporations might not have existed, or had they existed, they might not have had such sternly 'modern' design policies. The studio interiors of Broadcasting House, like the stations and rolling-stock [see **Plate 46**] of the Piccadilly Line, should therefore be seen as monuments not only to new technologies, but also to a transitional condition of British society which will not happen again.

Look at the photograph of the exterior of Broadcasting House [Plate 36] and the photographs of the interior [Plates 44–45 and filmstrips 1–5]. Do you detect an anomaly in the treatment of exterior and interior?

● The difference in style between the outside (public) styling of Broadcasting House and the interior (professional staff) decoration is so marked that it raises some obvious questions about the relationship of 'culture' and 'technology'. Even though Val Myer worked in Neo-Georgian for reasons beyond the BBC's control, What else could the BBC have looked like? For instance, there is no reason why it could not have looked like contemporary progressive institutions such as Gropius's Bauhaus or Le Corbusier's Cité de Refuge or adopted the favoured design policy of public utilities like the London Underground or the TVA—the models existed for imitation. Yet, perhaps because of its peculiarly sensitive position in society, the BBC was pleased to present a 'conservative' impression as its public face. ●

Conclusion

The adventures in mechanical and electrical environmental controls which have been chronicled in this unit have been regarded at various times with enthusiasm and disapproval, have been seen as the salvation of architecture or its destruction, and have now become a matter of general concern because of uncertainty about the future and the capacity of our energy supplies—the proliferation of the domestic package air-conditioners discussed in Part 2 section two is one of the causes of the more or less severe power failures in New York, every summer, just when air-conditioning is most needed.

The constantly escalating demand for fuels and water has raised understandable doubts whether this kind of environmental management can be supported much longer. On the other hand, the increased comfort, convenience and cleanliness it has brought into buildings represent a human good that even convinced ecologists seem unwilling to give up. Yet however one strikes the balance of good and evil in the last century of mechanical and electrical services, there seems to be one undoubted human gain that should be worth preserving: the ability to make a factual assessment of the environmental performance of buildings.

Before the mid-nineteenth century neither the need nor the ability really existed. Most parts of the world had arrived at environmentally tolerable vernacular building types and constructional methods. Importation of other countries' vernaculars produced predictably undesirable effects—hence Alexander Pope's commonsensical sneer at fashionable country-house owners who were 'proud to catch cold at a Venetian door'. But industrialization produced building types—mills, factories, board-schools—for which there were no vernacular precedents environmentally, while at the same time it produced new and untried machinery by which their environmental defects might be made good.

For these new techniques of heating, lighting and ventilating there was in the first place only one operating rule—thrift—that is to say, greed, meanness, profitability and the cold calculus of institutional charity. These, inevitably, led to stress and ill-health and—less directly—to the factory and public health acts. The medical men who served as inspectors in the enforcement in these acts became the first body of skilled environmentalists, possessed of at least a coarse statistical knowledge of the relationship between health and environmental conditions.

The law, armed with their knowledge and that of engineers, soon began to modify the simple-minded operations of capitalist greed. An unhealthy worker is an inefficient worker. Pollution comes from the inefficient—and therefore unprofitable—combustion of fuels. Those clients who wanted to know what they were getting for their money were soon asking questions that conventionally trained architects could not answer (and still cannot). The more desperate the client's environmental needs, the more innovative the processes offered by mechanical and electrical services consultants, the more specific had to be the information accompanying the proposed design.

Thus it came about that in an historic document of 1907 Willis Carrier became the first man to write a guarantee of the thermal and atmospheric performance of a building. Traditionally all that had been guaranteed had been the quality of materials and workmanship and this, with luck, might give some warranty of environmental quality or might not. But a client whose whole profitability might depend on minute variations in humidity or temperature needed stronger assurances, and for the Huguet Silk Mills in New York State, Carrier was prepared to guarantee that under such and such a set of climatic conditions he could give a temperature of 70°F and a humidity of 85% or that in other circumstances he could give the same humidity without going more than 5°F above outside temperature.

To make such an unprecedented offer Carrier needed to know not only the behaviour of his own plant, but also that of the building it was to serve, and quite a lot about the local climate. Most of this information was only just becoming available, and the maths to handle it was being made up by men like Carrier as they went along. Similar things were happening in the field of lighting, though it was not until the thirties that quantifiable standards for levels of illumination for different human tasks could be offered—the IES standards in the USA were promulgated first in 1936, the German *Normen* a year earlier. Both would be regarded as dangerously crude by today's standards, but they have already altered the appearance of buildings, since the establishment of the minimum '2% daylight factor' (measure of natural lighting devised by artificial lighting engineers) also establishes the minimum size of windows for different sizes of rooms in familiar buildings such as schools.

Inevitably the proliferation of these studies has bred accompanying cohorts of experts and further affected the practice of building design. Most mechanical and electrical services consultant are, for good and obvious reasons, likely to be electrical engineers by training, and their backgrounds—educational, social and cultural—are likely to be totally different from those of the architects whom they advise. Their basic disciplines are usually analytical and mathematical and contain little that architects would recognize as 'design'. Their expertise in measuring and estimating the performance of buildings tends therefore to be regarded with hostility by some architects, who believe that their creative freedoms are being whittled away.

Admittedly, some of these consultants have become wise and valued counsellors to the architectural profession, especially those who have grown up through the amateur and pioneering phases, like the legendary Oscar Faber, 'the father of mechanical and electrical services in England'. None, however, has seemed ready to take the kind of design initiatives nor the kind of design responsibilities that architects do. One never hears of an electrical engineer designing a building with an architect as 'spatial consultant', nor even does one find that Willis Carrier ever told an architect that he had designed a building in the wrong way to get maximum benefit from his air-conditioning. Rather he would accept the design as presented to him, and bend his great technological gifts to making his system work, at whatever cost, within the architect's framework. Had he not been of this turn of mind, he would undoubtedly have told Wallace Harrison exactly what Le Corbusier told him—that the glass walls must have a *brise-soleil* in order to reduce air-conditioning costs.

This attitude of assumed commercial humility ('I'm only paid to advise') may have bolstered some architectural egos and may have made possible one or two works of pure architectural art, but it is difficult to see how it has benefited the practice of architecture in general, or that it has benefited the human race at large as much as it should. Worst of all, it has allowed architects, who generally knew little enough of mechanical technology when it began, to go on knowing just as little ever since, and to excuse themselves for the ecological consequences of their own environmental ignorance by blaming it all on a mythical monster known as 'High Technology'. There is still a 'Problem of the Machine' to be solved, even if it is not the purely cultural one supposed by European architects in the thirties.

Appendix

1 Letter from Le Corbusier to Senator Warren Austin (see **Figure 6**)

Paris, December 4th, 1947.

The Honorable Senator Warren Austin,
President of the Commission of the
Site Planning Committee,
Lake Success, New York.

Dear Senator Austin:

On the 19th of November, I sent you a letter referring you to the text of the *Architectural Forum* which stated that Mr. Harrison had planned that the buildings would be equipped with large glass panes set in aluminium frames; these glass panes would be double, spaced one foot apart; in this space there would be circulated hot air in winter and cold air in summer, a procedure which would prevent excessive heat in summer and would allow solar heat to penetrate in winter.

I also informed you that this was my invention of 1929 called 'neutralizing wall', invented for the Ministry of Light Industries, which I was building at that time in Moscow. This invention was rejected by the Soviet authorities and my building was equipped with the traditional heating system using radiators. Moreover, I reminded you that in 1936 I established in collaboration with a group of Brazilian architects the plans for the Ministry of National Education Building in Rio de Janeiro, which was built during the war by my disciple Oscar Niemeyer. This building was equipped with 'brise-soleil' (sun-breakers, a form of sun control). The 'brise-soleil' was a solution I had found about 1929 for North Africa and which since then I have applied under various circumstances. In my letter of November 19th, I stated the following conclusions:

'My strong belief, Mr. Senator, is that it is senseless to build in New York, where the climate is terrible in the summer, large glass areas which are not equipped with a "brise-soleil." I say this is dangerous, very seriously dangerous!'

In the same letter of November 19th, I wrote you in a postscript that in agreement with Mr. Missenard, vice-regent of the *Institut Français Pour Les Recherches Humaines* (of which the late Dr. Carrel was president) that I would send you a very detailed report. I shall now give you briefly the exact conclusions dealing with this problem on which Mr. Missenard and I have agreed. Mr. Senator, please do not consider this problem beyond your comprehension because it appears to be too technical. The responsibility of building the United Nations Headquarters is grave, and I want to repeat once more that there is real danger involved in building large glass areas without 'brise-soleil' on the East River.

Fig. One.—Necessity of a 'neutralizing wall' for the construction of the United Nations Headquarters at New York.

Figure 6 Le Corbusier, illustration from letter to Senator Warren Austin, 1950

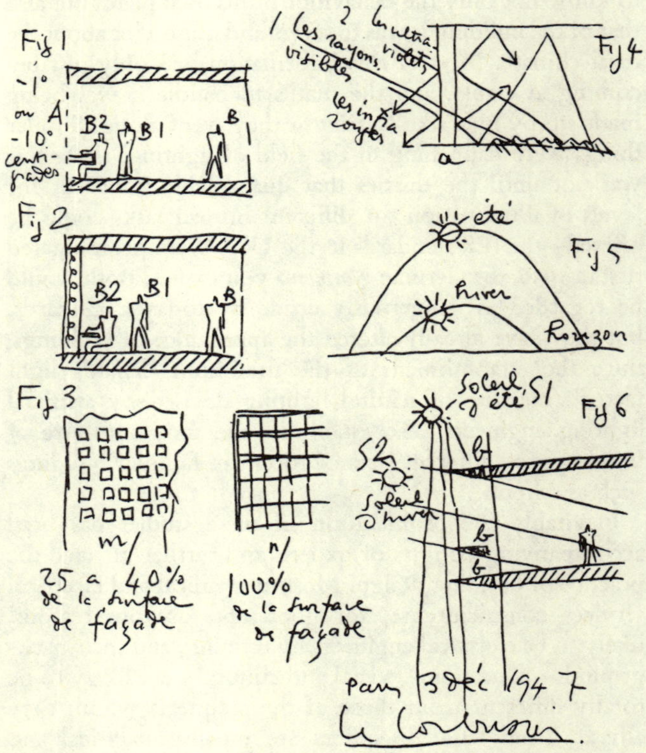

Fig. One shows the vertical section of one floor of a New York building. In A we have a window wall; the heating system provides an inside temperature of 20°C. (68°F.) from an outside temperature of 1°C. to —14°C. (33° to 6°F.). B represents a person enjoying relative comfort. B_1 and B_2 represent two people who are in an intolerable position surrounded by hot air but feeling intense cold.

Why this feeling of intense cold? Because (physical law) a body radiates heat to places colder than itself; consequently, here B_1 and B_2 radiate their own heat to the glass and their discomfort is so great that they will be unable to work. Hence, if these people are employed in the United Nations on the East River (directors, editors, accountants, typists, etc.) they will not be able to fill their jobs and the entire Secretariat of the United Nations will be incapacitated much more seriously than they were at Lake Success because of artificial light. This is extremely grave. It is decisive. One has no right to admit even once such an alternative.

Fig. Two.—A vertical section of the same room. This time there is a set of double glass panes separated by 8 to 10 cm (3–4 inches); between the panes hot air is circulated, creating the 'neutralizing wall'. This way the inside glass surface has ceased to be cooling. Consequently, the people B, B_1 and B_2 do not radiate their body heat towards the glass pane; B_1 and B_2 are now comfortable, and the work of the United Nations on the East River will be done under normal conditions.

Fig. Three.—m/ represents a façade of a part of a New York skyscraper with windows (25–40 per cent. of the surface); n/ represents a façade of a skyscraper of the project on the East River with a window-wall (100 per cent. of the surface).

In m/ you know that the working conditions are very conducive to fatigue in the present New York skyscrapers from June to September because of the intense New York heat.

In n/ the working conditions will be intolerable, of this we must be convinced, we must be sure, and we should be afraid. We must do what is necessary to prevent such a result.

Fig. Four.—Sunlight may be divided into:

1—visible rays;
2—ultra-violet rays;
3—infra-red rays;
4—miscellaneous rays.

Glass rejects the ultra-violet and infra-red rays. The visible rays penetrate, but as soon as they come into contact with any opaque body (called a black body), these rays are changed into heat which radiate in all directions but which is retained in the building.

Let us consider the summer months in connection with the 100 per cent. glass surface; the effect of these rays inside the building will be serious.

But Mr. Harrison declared: 'We shall circulate cold air between the two glass surfaces.' This cold air will have no effect on the visible rays going through the glass wall (100 per cent.). (One cannot cool rays.)

Do they hope to cool the glass area A so that it would become a radiator of cold? That is senseless; a fantastic quantity of refrigerant would be necessary (which would be very expensive); also the glass, a, is by definition a poor conductor. Therefore, there is no other solution than that of the brise-soleil, the explanation of which follows:

Figs. Five and Six.—The high summer sun S_1 has its rays broken by the brise-soleil b. The sun does not touch the windows nor does it reach the interior of the building, thus leaving the employees in complete comfort behind a 100 per cent. glass surface.

In winter when the sun S_2 is low on the horizon; it penetrates far into the building, bringing light, warmth and optimism.

This, Mr. Senator, is the physical truth:

1 It is indispensable to create a 'neutralizing wall' (an invention of Le Corbusier) to assure comfort in the working conditions of personnel behind window walls during the winter.
2 To equip the window wall with a brise-soleil to assure the comfort of the personnel during working hours during the summer.
3 The window wall allows a free disposition of rooms, the optimum use of space (the last modern conquest of steel and concrete).
4 One cannot make window walls without a '*neutralizing wall*' *and a* '*brise-soleil*' (just as one cannot make an automobile with a powerful motor without adequate brakes, etc.).

Mr. Senator, here are logical reasons which give your indisputable arguments which will aid you in making a decision regarding this problem. An error made by the United Nations in this direction could have serious consequences.

Most respectfully yours,
Le Corbusier.

(From *Architectural Review*, July 1950, pp. 69–71)

2 The Royal Victoria Hospital, Belfast and the Larkin Building, Buffalo

The less progressive in architectural style, but more advanced environmentally of the two, is the Royal Victoria Hospital in Belfast, Northern Ireland. At face-value, the credit for its design goes straightforwardly to the Birmingham architectural firm of Henman and Cooper, with Henry Lea as their engineering consultant, but a fog of rumour has always surrounded the design, because local pride insists that the whole concept is too original to chime with the rest of Henman and Cooper's work, and at first sight it must appear strange that in a city where the forced ventilation of ships was a technological habit, and where Samuel Cleland Davidson's Sirocco works was producing some of the world's most advanced centrifugal fans, neither influence should have had any apparent direct effect upon the design. Davidson's, it is clear, were responsible for the design, installation and subsequent maintenance of the heating and ventilation machinery, and if their influence on the architectural concept was not direct, it could still have operated more obliquely through Davidson's own business and social connections. Shipping and ship-building interests were strongly represented on the hospital's board of management (as on most other things in Belfast) and the suspicion that some of them may have talked the architects into the final bulk form of the building is heightened by thinly veiled accusations that the discussion at the Royal Insttiute of British Architects which followed the presentation of the design by the architects, was rigged and deliberately talked out of time by the scheme's supporters in order to prevent awkward questions being asked.

Be all this as it may, there can be no doubt about the propriety of making a public presentation of the design in the architectural profession's highest forum in Britain, because it represents a level of mechanical innovation and originality of plan that would have been hard to equal anywhere at the time. Within the work of Henman and Cooper themselves, the progress of innovation is clear enough. In their design for the Birmingham General Hospital in 1893, they had applied William Key's Plenum system of ventilation to a hospital organised on the traditional pavilion plan. This was an illogical and wasteful solution because the whole hygienic motivation of the use of separate pavilions had been to promote good natural ventilation between windows and other openings on opposite sides of relatively tall narrow buildings, such as survive in many British hospitals from the last century. With forced ventilation of any sort, this type of planning became unnecessary, and the large amount of external surface relative to the floor area would lead to a relatively uneconomic waste of heat. To get full advantage from the Plenum system, a much more compact plan would obviously be required, with as much as possible of the accommodation packed into a single structural volume (in order to avoid heat wastage from underground ducts between separate buildings).

These desiderata were fully achieved in the Royal Victoria Hospital, Belfast, where the maximum compactness of plan is combined with a minimum length of duct. Nevertheless, the duct is one of the most monumental in the history of environmental engineering; a brick tunnel with a concrete floor, over five hundred feet long and nine feet wide, twenty feet deep at the input end, tapering upwards to only six feet deep at the downstream end. As may be deduced, this was no high-velocity system—a set of steam engines operated by waste steam from the hospital laundry's boilers drove a pair of slow-turning axial flow fans on a common shaft in an engine house at the input end of the duct. The output from these fans fed together into a Y-branched inlet, and thus into the duct, up which warm air moved at a little over walking pace in winter, and cool air somewhat faster in summer.

From the giant duct, the air was fed into distributor channels (also of brick and concrete) opening off the left-hand wall of the duct and high under its ceiling. From the distributors, the air rose through risers in the walls of the wards and was delivered through openings above head level into the wards on either side. For the wards were laid out in a tight parallel plan, with only party walls between them, single storey, and served by a common corridor the same width as the main duct and running its full length. Since the wards were butted up solidly edge to edge, and the intervening walls were not available for windows, the wards were lit by long lay-lights on either side of their pitched roofs, and by arched openings onto the balconies at the end. At the corridor end, kitchens, operating theatres, private wards, were fitted between the entrances to the wards. Thus the whole medical work space of the hospital was packed into a densely occupied single-storey block, divided into rooms, all top lit, that received tempered air from registers above head level, and disposed of foul air through slots in the skirting around the perimeter of the rooms, whence it descended into extract ducts parallel to the input distributors, and finally left the building through vertical risers terminating in the louvered lanterns, one at the end of each ward, which are a conspicuous feature of all external views of the building.

The degree of control designed by Davidson into the air-supply system was rigorous by the standards of the time (1903) and made ingenious use of the comparatively crude technology available. Air, on entering through window-type openings in the ends of the engine-house, was pulled through hanging curtains of coconut fibre robes kept moist by sprinklers in the roof of the filter-chamber (this water could be warmed in winter to prevent freezing). Cleaned of soot, smuts and other impurities for which the Belfast atmosphere was notorious, the air then passed through batteries of heating-coils before entering the fans and being propelled up the duct. In order to prevent excessive temperature drop during its relatively leisurely journey to the far end of the duct, the air received extra heat in winter from a booster pipe running its full length and from further coils of pipe in the entrance to each distributor.

This system, intended first to provide warmed and cleaned air to all the medical and surgical areas of the hospital, brought with it an additional benefit. Because the outside air was dirtiest in winter, that was also the season when the sprinkler system to moisten the filters was most used. But the winter was also the time when there was the biggest difference in external and internal air temperatures —air entering the system below freezing would leave it at a temperature in the sixties Fahrenheit—and thus the greatest reduction in relative humidity, in any system that did not make good the deficiency in the water-vapour content of the air. But this deficiency was, crudely, made good by the sprinkler system, more or less in direct ratio to need, because the colder the day, the more soot would be pumped into the Belfast atmosphere, and the more water would be run through the sprinklers and taken up by the air that passed through the ropes.

Had this topping-up of the relative humidity of the atmosphere been left to happy accident, there would be no point in enquiring whether the Royal Victoria Hospital has a place among pioneer air conditioning systems, but it was never left entirely to accident. From the beginning, Davidson had intended some form of humidity control, and before 1920, if medical memories are to be trusted, it became the practice to observe the humidity of the air in the wards night and morning, by the normal wet-bulb/dry-bulb thermometer technique, and instruct the engineman to regulate the flow of water over the filter ropes accordingly. This immediately puts the historical argument on a different footing, for as soon as the humidity of the air is consciously regulated, along with the temperature and cleanliness, then there was air-conditioning in the strict sense laid down by Stuart Cramer in his fundamental patents of 1906

I have used the term 'air-conditioning' to include humidifying and air cleaning and heating and ventilation.

or as emphasised much later by Willis Carrier

...added to the control of humidity are the control of temperature by either heating or cooling, purification of the air by washing or filtering the air, and the control of air-motion and ventilation.

But, since these conditions were achieved before the conscious art of conditioning air had been even given a name, and may not have become fully deliberate until after the art had become conscious, the position of the Royal Victoria Hospital among the pioneers of air-conditioning remains a little difficult to assess without becoming involved in semantic niceties. On the other hand it does seem true to say that it must have been the first major building to be air-conditioned for human comfort—earlier installations were exclusively industrial, and the deliberate air-conditioning of cinemas in the US came only in 1922, which seems definitely to be later than the beginning of conscious and continuous humidity control at the Royal Victoria Hospital.

In any case, the importance of the hospital in the history of architecture lies in its total adaptation in section and plan to the environmental system employed. What makes it even more interesting historically is that more than one environmental system is employed, the architecture changing to suit, for a great part of the accommodation to the 'right' of the great corridor and duct was not served by the conditioning system, which was reserved for areas occupied by the sick. The areas occupied by the fit—office-workers, nurses off-duty, etc.—had conventional heating by gas fires and conventional ventilation by means of opening windows, since it was known that the fit would insist on controlling their own environment, even if the sick could not.

What is immediately striking about these areas of conventional environmental control is that they also revert to conventional architectural form in plan and section; they are relatively tall (five full storeys) and thin, so that they both catch the wind, and allow it to pass through any random combination of opened windows on either side of the block. They are, in fact, close relations of the pavilioned ward blocks that Henman and Cooper, and the rest of the profession, had become accustomed to design. The external massing of the various parts of the hospital thus gives direct 'expression' to two different kinds of environmental management, a low, top-lit format corresponding to mechanical systems, and a tall, side-lit format to natural systems.

The external aspect of the Royal Victoria Hospital also demonstrates with painful clarity the total irrelevance of detailed architectural 'style' to the modernity of the functional and environmental parts. As will now be clear, the hospital is extremely 'modern' and ahead of its time in its environmental controls; and it is also very modern in the way the parts are functionally disposed along a spine corridor without regard for axial symmetry—in these aspects of plan and circulation it approximates to the advanced practices of some thirty years later, and in the implied extensibility of its plan along the line of the corridor, it is still of interest to proponents of 'indeterminate' architecture some sixty years later. But in its detailing, in what its designers doubtless regarded as its 'art architecture' it belongs dismally and irrevocably to a conception of 'Welfare' architecture fathered by the London School Board some forty years before, a style already thoroughly discounted and out of fashion among consciously progressive architects of 1900.

Without doubt it is this depressingly un-modish exterior that has caused the Royal Victoria Hospital to be universally overlooked by historians of the Modern Movement until the last few years. It is not mentioned by any of the historian-protagonists of Functionalism; it receives not even a footnote in Pevsner's *Pioneers of the Modern Movement*, in spite of the fact that in all except the purely stylistic sense it was far more modern and far more pioneering than anything that had been designed by Walter Gropius, the hero-figure of the book, before 1914. . . . These lacks in historiographical method appear very clearly in the literature about the only building contemporary with the Royal Victoria Hospital whose environmental architecture can really be compared with it in radicalism and ingenuity—Frank Lloyd Wright's Larkin Office building in Buffalo, New York. No one doubts that it was one of the early masterpieces of pioneer, modern architecture, and if Wright had designed nothing afterwards he would still have held a strong place among the fathers of twentieth-century design. Because its exterior was expertly pleasing and conformed to the stripped classical taste favoured by the other pioneers, especially the Europeans like Perret, Garnier, Behrens and Gropius, the Larkin building finds a natural place in the history books, unlike the Royal Victoria Hospital. But like the hospital, it has a neatly equivocal place in the environmental history of its times, for, as Wright himself put it:

The Larkin administration building was a simple cliff of brick hermetically sealed (one of the first 'air-conditioned' buildings in the country) to keep the interior space clear of the poisonous gases in the smoke from the New York Central trains that puffed along beside it.

This is a strong claim; most historians have either passed it over as if unnoticed, or—what is worse—repeated it without the quotation marks which Wright knowingly put round the words 'air-condition'. . . . Historical and critical writing has tended to concentrate exclusively on the felicity of its interior spaces and their relationship to the great monumental volumes of the exterior, without observing that the system of environmental management mediates crucially between interior and exterior form. Not only is the use of a vast single vessel of space ringed with balconies almost a necessity given the then state of artificial ventilation, but it was a flash of inspiration, about the disposition of the services to achieve that ventilation, that gave the magisterial form of the exterior. Wright again:

But not until the contract had been let to Paul Mueller and the plaster model of the building stood completed on the big detail board at the centre of the Oak Park draughting room, did I get the articulation I finally wanted. The solution that had hung fire came in a flash. I took the next train to Buffalo to try and get the Larkin Company to see that it was worth thirty thousand dollars more to build the stair-towers free of the central block, not only as an independent stair-towers for communication and escape, but also as air-intakes for the ventilating system.

The Larkin Building no longer exists, having been demolished in 1950, but the surviving paper evidence—including a few photographs taken during demolition—serve to confirm how crucial was that flash of inspiration about where to put the services, in giving the elusive articulation that was afterwards to make the design so famous. As is well known, the basic *parti* of Wright's layout surrounds the galleried central space with four corner towers, and flanking entrance unit, lying on the transverse axis to one side. Much of the inner wall surface of the working galleries, including the backs of the solid balustrades, was given over to modular filing cabinets, and the external windows, closed against the unwelcome atmosphere outside, were set high under the ceilings of each tier, above the filing cabinets.

The internal atmosphere was serviced as follows: air from well above the external pollutants was drawn down capacious ducts in the blank walls of the corner towers, at the sides of the staircases, as Wright indicates. In the basement it was cleaned and heated, or after the installation of the Kroeschell refrigerating plant in 1909, cooled—but never humidity-controlled, and hence Wright's judicious quotation-marks around the words 'air-conditioned' (in the town where Carrier was perfecting humidity control he had better be careful!). The tempered air was then blown up riser ducts in the massive blank brick panels on the exterior walls immediately adjacent to the stair-towers, and distributed floor by floor through input registers on the backs of the downstand beams under the balustrades of the balconies. The same blank brick panels also contain the exhaust ducts through which vitiated air is extracted, and a third duct-space in the panel houses pipes and wiring and other ancillaries. Throughout the interior, extracts are marked by a characteristic and much-used Wrightian device—a pattern of hollow bricks forming a coarse grille, around which even the earliest photographs show the typical staining that commonly marks an exhaust.

Neat as these usages may be, and monumental as their external consequences may be, the Larkin Building, like the Royal Victoria Hospital, must be judged a design whose final form was imposed by the method of environmental management employed, rather than one whose form derived from the exploitation of an environmental method.

The Royal Victoria Hospital and its innumerable predecessors in the realm of 'welfare architecture' for industrialized mass-societies, often present the image of new functional needs and mechanical possibilities bursting through a crust of conventionally conceived architectural forms, whereas in the Larkin Building, the transformation of the exterior, both in detail and in mass, appears to be keeping pace with transformation of the interior economy of the building-type. Thus Wright, in the Larkin Building design, serves as a bridge between the history of modern architecture as commonly written—the progress of structure and external form—and a history of modern architecture understood as the progress of creating human environments.

(Edited extract from: Reyner Banham, *The Architecture of the Well-tempered Environment*, Architectural Press, 1970, pp. 75–91)

3 Recent Progress in the Electric Lighting of Buildings by John Slater

A paper on this subject was delivered by Mr. John Slater, B.A., F.R.I.B.A., at the rooms of the Royal Institute of British Architects on Monday evening. The room was lighted by incandescent lamps of the Swan, Edison, Lane-Fox, and Maxim types, supplied with power from an accumulator invented by Messrs. Sellon and Voelekmar, and which stood in the room. The meeting was crowded, and the lecturer's address and experiments were followed with evident interest. Mr. Slater referred to the evidence given before a select committee of the House of Commons, but three years since, by such scientists as Sir William Thomson and Professor Tyndall, as to the impracticability of sub-dividing the electric light for domestic use, in illustration of the revolution which the discoveries of the last three years have effected in the opinions of scientific men as to the sphere of usefulness of the electric light. This revolution, he showed, was mainly due to the invention of incandescent lighting, which might be defined to be the unlimited power of concentrating large quantities of heat into small foci without consuming the heated body, which thus became a stable and unchanging point of light, in contradistinction to the arc lights, in which the glowing material was continually disintegrating and burning away. The incandescent systems of electric lighting were based on the fact that, if preserved from combustion, carbon is practically infusible, and the chief difficulties in the way of making incandescent lamps lay in the fact that it was necessary to inclose in an exhausted glass globe an extremely thin filament of carbon, which must be in electrical contact with wires outside the globe, and which must be able to stand an enormously high temperature. Messrs. Swan, Lane-Fox, Edison, and Maxim had overcome these difficulties in different ways, each of which was described in detail. Incandescent lamps could be used with almost all kinds of dynamo machines, but they could also be worked with an invention which, as a practical means of supplying electricity, must be regarded as the outcome of the past year, but which would be epoch-making in the history of electric lighting—viz., the storage batteries, or accumulators of electrical energy. That room was lighted by means of force stored in one of the newest forms of these accumulators—that of Messrs. Sellon and Voelckmar, so that no engine was necessary; and the lecturer showed by experiment that it was quite possible to shut off or utilise cells in this accumulator, so as to diminish or increase brilliancy of the lamps at pleasure, and also to extinguish any one without affecting the other lights. The economic value of incandescent lighting was one of the most important points to be considered, and although at present the data upon which to found an opinion were but scanty, the cases in which the details of cost had been most accurately worked out tended to show that the economic value of the new means of illumination had been, if anything, underrated. The readiness with which the incandescent lights lent themselves to any scheme of decoration was one of their chief attractions. It would be undesirable to follow on the lines of gas-fittings, as the conditions were so completely altered, but points of light could be placed wherever they were required, and there was no fear of blackening ceilings and decorations or of setting fire to the most easily-ignited materials. The progress of this system of lighting had been so rapid that architects had as yet had no time to turn their attention to its decorative capabilities, but when they did so, they would find it fulfil every requirement for perfect lighting. Mr. Slater then alluded to the arc light systems, in which, although less progress had been made during the past year, the sphere of usefulness had become more clearly defined, and the Mansion House was a good example of their adaptation to rooms of an exceptionally large size. If these large lights could be concealed and their rays reflected downwards from a large screen or a white ceiling, a very pleasant and diffused light would be obtained, and the slight irregularities, due for the most part to the carbons, would be much less perceptible. Simplicity of construction was the great thing to be aimed at in these lamps, and the Weston arc lamp was a good example of their newest form, and this might be termed a strictly electrical lamp, as contrasted with a mechanical one. The great difficulty with which these arc lamps had to contend was in the nature of the carbons, in the manufacture of which but little improvement had taken place; but he looked to competition to effect as decided a development in this detail as it had recently done in others. The social aspects of this question were very important. These concerned the distribution and measurement of the electricity, the conditions necessary for reconciling the rights of the consumer and of the purveyor, and the risks to be guarded against. For electricity to compete with gas as a general means of illumination, it must offer as many facilities as its rival; and the Edison installation in Holborn, and that of the Swan lamps at the Savoy Theatre showed practically that this condition was complied with. After describing these installations, the author explained the various methods of laying the mains, connecting the branches and arranging the lamps so that all were perfectly independent of each other, and showed how the strength of the current in the mains was cleverly regulated in proportion to the amount of work that it had to do. Perfect insulation throughout was the great desideratum, and if this point were always carefully kept in view, the dangers of electric lighting would be reduced to a minimum. Considerable attention had been given to this matter in America, and the Board of Fire Underwriters of New York had framed a code of regulations bearing on the subject. The Crystal Palace Exhibition was an exceptional case, as the installations were temporary, and the risks such as could not possibly occur in a well-devised permanent arrangement. A mode of measuring the current by a meter into which a portion of the current was diverted, had been ingeniously worked out by Mr. Edison. Mr. Slater then referred to the importance of the subject to architects, and concluded his paper thus:—The progress of electrical science is the most striking feature of the latter part of this nineteenth century, and the day is not far distant when we shall find a certain acquaintance with the subject of electric science a necessity for us architects in our every-day work, unless we wish to be entirely in the hands of the men whom we employ. Science has captured the lightning it is true, but it is scarcely tamed yet; let us beware that we do not attempt to deal with this new servant ignorantly. Electricity is a new power given into our hands to work out, and it behoves us to study its nature and advantages and to guard against its risks and dangers, and to learn to use it, together with the older means at our disposal, in accordance with the maxim 'Usui civium, decori urbium.'

In the discussion which followed, Mr. Swan, of Newcastle, said there was a distinct economy, light for light, in the use of incandescent lamps over gas. For example, 2cwt. of coal, if carbonised in a gas-retort, would produce, during one hour, 1,000 cubic feet of gas and 3,000 candle-power. The same coal could be utilised as fuel to an engine so as to furnish 100 horse-power during the hour, and as each horse-power was equal to the production of at least 200 candles of illumination in incandescent lamps, the total power of the coal was, roughly speaking, 20,000 candles for electricity against 3,000 for gas. Against this, however, must be set off on the side of gas, the value of the residual products, which were now regarded as worth about 1s. per 1,000 cubic feet of gas, thereby reducing its net cost from 2s. 9d. to 1s. 9d. per thousand. If, however, this drawback was estimated at one-half, it would be seen that the absolute relative cost of the two sources of illumination was at the least as 20 is to 6 in favour of the incandescent system. He did not think that the public were menaced with a new monopoly in this form of lighting, as the free competition of inventors would procure a remedy for that danger; the real peril was lest legislative restriction should hamper and impede the development of invention.

Mr. George Lane-Fox declared that the alleged dangers of shock and fire from electric lighting were mere myths conjured up in the imaginations of gas and insurance companies. There had been, doubtless, a few accidents from the new source of light, but these were very slight compared with the fatalities that attended the early use of gas. In both cases they were due to the ignorance and negligence of those using the new illuminator. As to risk of physical shock, there might be some in the large arc lights, but the persons supplying incandescent lamp-power had every inducement to reduce the force of the tension to a point absolutely imperceptible to the human body. There was indeed no advantage in using a high tension: with a low one the light was more easily controlled and divided, and was more economical. In the early days of gas-lighting the average loss by leakage was 50 per cent. This was presently reduced to 30 per cent., and now was considered wasteful if it exceeded 3. With the electric light engineers started with the experience gained in telegraphy, and the loss through negligence and want of insulation would probably be much less.

Mr. C. F. Hayward mentioned that, in the experimental lighting of Godalming it was attempted to utilise the water-power from a mill on the Wey for driving the electric motors. This failed, not from any defect in the system, but because allowance had not been made for fluctuations in the stream through floods and drought. The lights consequently failed, but Messrs. Siemens were called in, and fixed an engine, and the lighting was now regarded as satisfactory by the tradesmen, although somewhat more expensive than gas.

(From *Building News*, 19, May 1882, pp. 600 ff.)

4 On the opening of the Universum Kino, 1931, by Eric Mendelsohn

Cinemas?
Pictures, theatre of motion!
Motion is life.
Real life is genuine, simple and true,
Therefore no affection, no sentimentality.
Not in the pictures, not on the screen, not in building.
Show what it contains, what it is and what its own limitations are. Theatre? Not at all!
Elevator for the screen when the Sketch is succeeded by the film.
Advertisement tower-Artificial architecture?—On the contrary!
Ventilation outlets (change of air, three times an hour) go straight out in the direction of the Kurfürstendamm:
For there we are: Universum—the whole world—the façades of a palace?—and the profitability: shops make money, offices vivify the scene and procure a public.
Porch entrance for high society?
Mouth opened widely and flooded with light, decorated in splendour.
For—you are to go in, everyone—into life, to the film, to the pay box!
Cathedral cupolas? What for! Tortoise-shaped roof, projecting curves of the sloping ceiling, going towards the screen wall.
Ah! Camera!
Right!
Screen—the outside world.
Pictures—the bright life, tears, circus and moonlight at the sea-side.
We spectators—thousand, two thousand retinas, which suck up and reflect, each one happy or living an experience.
Thus, no rococócastle for Buster Keaton, no stucco pastries for Potemkin and Scapa Flow.
But, also, no fear!
No sober reality, no claustrophobia of life—wear brain acrobats—Fantasy!
Fantasy—but no lunatic asylum—dominated by space, colour and light.
Under the swinging circle of the foyer, the street disappears, under the conical beams of the ceiling lights, the haze of evening disappears.
Then—left or right pass by the beacon of the pay-box into the twilight of the passage—Here you surely meet 'them'.
Bend down in tension!
Compressor!
But then full speed.
All planes, curves and light waves flash from the ceiling to the screen through the medium of music into the flickering image—into the Universe.

(*Bauwelt*, 1961, nos. 41–42, p. 1184, translation D. Sharp, in *Modern Architecture and Expressionism*, London, 1966)

Unit 22
The Modern Flat

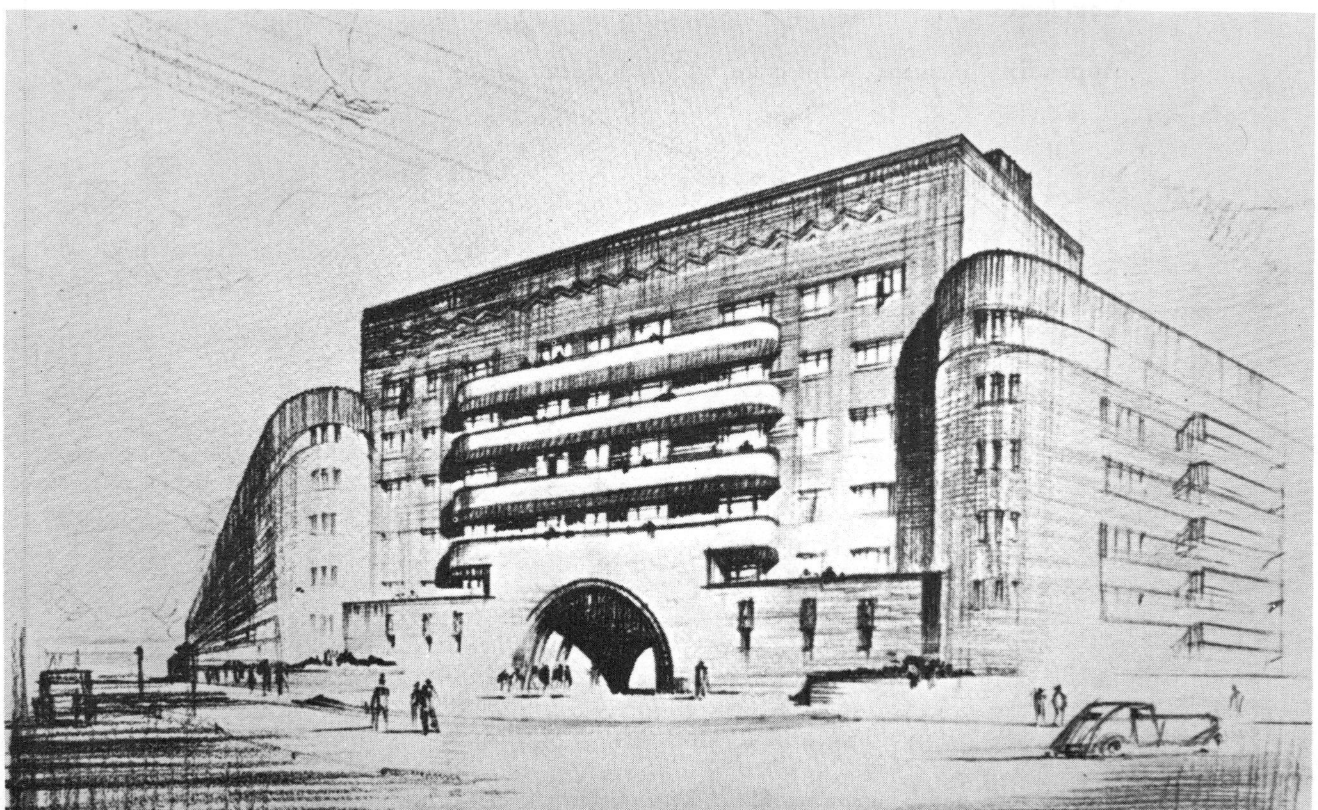

Unit 22 Contents

Half title page: artist's impression of L. H. Keay's Gerard Gardens, Christian Street, Liverpool (Liverpool City Libraries).

Introduction to Unit 22

It is only with some misgivings that I have decided to call this unit 'The Modern Flat', for it is not a straightforward account of creation–influence–imitation and the effect which this chain reaction had on flat design. Rather than that, its purpose is to take a step back from the arena where the modern battle of the styles was fought out and to survey more widely the general field of influences operating on housing policy and design in England in the early twentieth century. This has been done by continuing to examine the behind-the-scenes aspects of architecture which Reyner Banham initiated in Unit 21, his survey of the major service innovations and their effects on buildings.

I want to show how some of these services were applied to real situations where real peoples' lives were involved and where benefits and disadvantages can most easily be perceived and measured. To do this I have chosen to write about the flat. While it may not have been numerically the most popular form of housing in England it is important as the principal vehicle chosen by twentieth-century theorists as the solution to the housing problem. Because of this you must conceive of the flats treated in this unit as self-conscious forms of system-building peculiar to the needs of our era.

Part One is divided into three sections. This part is designed to show that, despite its identification with the twentieth century, the flat is not a building type peculiar to this age but has a number of historical precedents. It was in the nineteenth century that two of the most characteristic forms of flat building evolved: one of them was the working man's tenement; the other was the mansion house type. The first was often the creation of philanthropical bodies or commercial organizations with social-reformist persuasions. The second was a direct descendant of the Regent's Park terraces of John Nash.

The second section of Part One is an edited extract from F. R. S. Yorke's and Frederick Gibberd's *The Modern Flat* which analyses and categorizes the types and forms of the flat as they were perceived in the mid 1930s. This was a book of seminal importance in the history of modern architecture in England; yet, although both Yorke and Gibberd were clear enough thinkers, it is obvious that both men were seduced to argue irrationally by the power of the International Style doctrine. The book, and in particular this extract, provides an outstanding model for study and an insight into the pathology of the modernist mind of the 1930s. When you have read this section you should be able to apply Yorke and Gibberd's analytical principles to any flats you see.

Section 3 of Part One discusses the role of legislation in the creation of flats and describes the intentions and achievements of the London County Council's massive programme of flat building.

Part Two is a general survey of the influence of the Continent in English architectural affairs. First of all (Section 1), there was the importation of radical, new building technology into this country and (Section 2) then there was a less tangible import: the politico-stylistic controversy over the form and symbolism of the flat block. This was not at all an artificial issue for in the 1930s, housing—as much as economics today—was a live political issue. Section 3 of Part Two is concerned with the formulation of a European housing policy known as *Existenzminimum* (usually translated as 'dwellings for the lowest income') by the CIAM.

Part Three is the core of the unit and is a series of brief case studies of some important flat blocks of the 1930s. This is followed by the Conclusion and an Appendix contributed by the architect, W. A. Eden.

The problems involved with the existence of flats in England illuminate important aspects of the English attitude to modern architecture. It was over the question of 'How do we house these people?' that the modern architectural debate was fought out. In the debate the traditionalists brought the full force of the English reluctance to innovate (see Sir Reginald Blomfield in *Form and Function* No. 91) to bear on the spirited arguments of modernism represented by, for instance, Wells Coates (see *Form and Function* No. 113) who propagandized for the rejection of old forms and the invention of new ones entirely appropriate to the twentieth-century spirit and its material needs.

Because of the activities of the CIAM and activists like Coates, the International Style became almost inextricably involved with the cause of the flat. However, what this unit should make clear is that the International Style failed to create a durable aesthetic and was treated merely as a transient continental whim which could not possibly take root in England. History has endorsed the arguments of the traditionalists: firstly, the idea that only a *house* can be a *home* tended to diminish widespread enthusiasm for the flat as a building type and, on the other hand, a certain wariness about the political ramifications of building barracks for the disaffected and, worse still, dressing them up in the 'bolshevik' International Style worried local authorities. So marked was their aversion that in Liverpool even erstwhile architectural radicals like Lancelot Herman Keay were encouraged to practise in a more *moderne* than modern style. The paradox of this was that Keay adopted a style derived from the example of the Viennese *superblocks* which, while not International Style, were a more volatile political symbol than concrete, steel and glass could ever be.

In reading this unit you must try to be alive to the reality of the buildings which are being discussed. Remember at once that these are not the wild schemes of feverish-eyed dreamers but homes of ordinary people. Remember, too, the gulf between the architect's impression and the often less satisfactory reality. For instance, Lancelot Keay's early projects for St Andrew's Gardens [**Figure 31**] show heroic, futuristic blocks with cars whizzing around the place and the residents nobly perambulating like Athenians in their stoas, doubtless reflecting on what a fine place is this St Andrew's Gardens. Less than thirty years later, this workers' paradise could be described as 'brick littered waste-lands . . . scrofulous old walls, slatternly pavements and everywhere litter and mess.'[1]

It is, perhaps, significant that we are considering a period which saw the introduction of the miniature camera, and the widespread use of panchromatic film. The miniature camera encouraged the use of dramatic angles; panchromatic film is very flattering to the buildings illustrated in this unit (particularly those in the International Style). It does not show up stained rendering or rusty metal casements and indeed, so much does the style suit the film that it is possible that the one was created for the other! In the photographs there are beautiful contrasts of black and white, and sharp, crisp angles abounding everywhere combine to persuade the young architect of the 1930s to work in its clean, noble vein.

With this in mind you should consider the strong and necessary corrective to a too romantic and visual interpretation of the aesthetic of the International Style, apparent on pointing out that Connell, Ward and Lucas's Kent House [**Plate 89**] was not originally dazzlingly white but was once pink with royal blue trimmings and Maxwell Fry's Kensal House is not Corbusian ivory but pale green! (See film strip frame 8.)

AIMS OF UNIT 22

1 To show the evolution of the flat as a building type and to examine how it came to be regarded as the Modern Movement's solution to the housing problem.

2 To analyse the types of flat and their constituent parts.

3 To show the role of political factors in the public reaction to architecture.

4 To show the role of 'style' in creating an architectural ideology.

5 To assess the effects of structural and servicing innovations on flat design.

[1] *The Liverpool Echo*, 17 May 1965.

Part one The problem of the flat

1 The historical background and flats before the First World War

The etymology and the semantic origins of the word 'flat' are obscure, although its appears to have its origins in Scotland where it was used to mean the individual divisions of accommodation within a single house. This sense persists in Scotland up to the present day where a distinction is still made between a 'flatted house' and a 'tenement flat'.[1] During the early nineteenth century the word came to mean a suite of rooms or a whole floor in a building and it has by now matured into meaning a self-contained domestic unit within a larger structure.

When W. Shaw Sparrow wrote that a flat

> . . . should supply what a house gives—namely, proper facilities for entertaining, and quietude for the principal tenants, whose rooms, accordingly, when possible, should be isolated from the secondary rooms and from the servants' quarters.
>
> (W. Shaw Sparrow, *Flats, Urban Houses and Cottage Homes*, Hodder, n.d. (*c.* 1905), p. 9)

he was suggesting two things. The first is that the flat is a substitute for a house. It was this suggested reappraisal of modes of living to which time had given its sanction which caused the defenders of tradition to set up the cottage as a rival to the flat. This was the immediate reaction to the arrival of the 'continental' flat in England. The cottage home (which was not always as glamorous or as picturesque as it sounds) was set up in competition to the flat and was regarded by its supporter as tradition's stake in the housing of the future. The propagandists of the flat, on the other hand, were anxious to maintain that the flat-dweller need not be at a disadvantage when compared to the fellow who lived within his own four walls. This brings us to the second issue raised by W. Shaw Sparrow. Sparrow was the editor of *The Studio* and can be regarded as one of the magi of taste in the early part of this century. While the greater part of the emphasis in this unit will be on working-class flat schemes it is apparent on reading the extract from Sparrow's book that the earliest flats, while still, of course, built and occupied for reasons of economy and convenience, were intended both for the poor and the rich. It is this duality of purpose of the flat idea which characterizes it in its flourishing period. The early history of the flat divides clearly into two distinct traditions: the first is the development of the flats for the 'industrious' poor and the second is the grandiose mansion-house type of flat built in central London for the rich. It might seem a paradox that rich and poor lived in similar quarters but it is important to make it plain that the rich were able to buy their way out of many of the problems involved with flat living.

The propagandists of the flat often found it expedient to gloss over these problems, while the poor were restricted to their single floor dwelling with no garden and no recreation space, the rich most often used the flat only as an urban residence and retired to the country at the weekend where the fresh air absorbed would compensate for what they lacked in the week in their London flat. It was the same with servicing problems. The rich did not need to concern themselves with the problems of washing clothes in confined spaces, for they could afford to send out their dirty linen to commercial laundries. Similarly, they did not need to concern themselves with the preparation of meals in a small kitchen for, as any reader of an English novel written between 1890 and 1940 will know, the gentlemen lunched and dined at their clubs.

Of course, the idea that more than one family should live in one building is not a new one. In continental Europe political instability had necessitated the retention of defensive city walls for far longer than in England, where city defences had ceased to be built after the fifteenth century (see introduction to Units 5–6). The effect of this had been to put a premium on central urban space which gave the tradition of tenement flats in Europe their long pedigree. In the British Isles flats only became a solution to problems of space in Scotland and north-east England. In Edinburgh there are flats which date back to the seventeenth century and in Newcastle-upon-Tyne (where fortifications were retained for much .longer than the rest of England) there is an old tradition of workmen sharing dwellings. At Byker, for instance, an apparently ordinary working-man's cottage has, on close inspection, two front doors in tandem which serve two separate flats incorporated in the same building. Not only this, but there are more romantic interpretations of the history of the flat: the idea as such has existed for centuries among Oxford and Cambridge colleges where undergraduates and fellows have their 'rooms' in a common building and, again, in the London inns of court where the individual barristers' chambers correspond to the idea of the flat. In palaces too, courtiers had flats, and tenement blocks even existed on the Aventine in Rome as early as the fifth century BC.

Generally, however, England saw the appropriation of the flat to its domestic housing needs much later than Scotland and mainland Europe. Although, for the wealthy, there were bachelor flats such as The Albany (the old York House) existing as early as 1804 (Byron kept rooms there) the cause of flats for the working man in pressing need of accommodation only developed later in the century. The concern to house workers is the origins of the modern flat. The form which the solution took was the tenement block (as opposed to the 'flatted house' as at Byker); the majority of initiatives in this field took place in London but there were notable exceptions to the capital city's lead.

Perhaps the first tenement flats in England appeared in Birkenhead, Cheshire, and were built for the employees

[1] *Planning Our New Homes*, The Scottish Housing Advisory Committee. Edinburgh, 1945.

of the Birkenhead Dock Company in 1844–5. There were 324 separate dwellings in four-storey blocks, each one labelled with a gigantic letter of the alphabet to aid its identification, laid out on a triangular site bounded by Stewart Street, Ilchester Street and Stanley Road. Despite the association which the word 'tenement' now has with charity and philanthropy, these flats were not built for the destitute or the misplaced urban poor but were created to provide decent accommodation for ordinary working men and their families. The rents were not cheap at 3s 6d to 5s weekly, but for this the dock workers were provided with a self-contained flat offering a living room, two bedrooms, a scullery and a WC. Each flat was approached from a common stairway serving two flats on each floor.[1] Although the basic services were provided (there were water tanks, gas supply, dust chutes and drainage) it is salutary to consider how barbaric the sanitary conditions must have been. Reyner Banham pointed out in Unit 21 (pp. 12–13) that it was not so much the electric lift which made tall buildings possible, as the provision of lighting which produced neither dirt nor heat and the reliable water-borne waste disposal system. These services were necessary to satisfy the hygienic necessities of communal living and were not available in these model flats in Birkenhead.

Tenements for the industrious poor

Among the first flats to appear in London were built by the *Metropolitan Association for Improving the Conditions of the Industrious Poor* in Old St Pancras Road in 1848. In the same year, William Back built the Albert Family buildings for the *Metropolitan Association for Improving the Dwellings of the Poor* in Stepney. These were soon followed by the 'Model Dwellings for Families' built in Streatham Street, Bloomsbury by the *Society for Improving the Conditions of the Labouring Classes* in 1849.[2] The Streatham Street flats were designed by the architect Henry Roberts [**Plates 47–48**]. He created a scheme where fifty-four flats were arranged in five-storey blocks enclosing three sides of an open courtyard. Access to the individual flats, which had front doors quite the same as a house of 1849, was by open galleries supported, one above the other, by massive piers (**Figure 7**). Roberts also experimented with the idea of disguising a cottage to contain individual flats (rather in the tradition of Byker) and he exhibited two such examples at the Great Exhibition of 1851.

While at this time all the flat developments in London were undertaken by private societies, it was in Liverpool that the local authority first took on responsibility for creating housing. A commonplace now, this was unprecedented in the nineteenth century. The 1864 *Liverpool Sanitary Amendment Act* empowered the corporation to purchase compulsorily the insanitary 'courts' in slum areas and in one of these areas they constructed St Martin's Cottages, Everton, in 1869. It is an interesting semantic point that these first council flats in England were called 'cottages'; it seems that even in the experimental period of flat building authorities were a little wary of acknowledging that they were not building houses. Meanwhile, in London, the tradition of tenement building was given its greatest impetus in the early 1860s with the creation of *The Peabody Donation Fund* in 1862 and *The Improved Industrial Dwellings Company* in 1863. Peabody was an American Banker with philanthropical inclinations. He came to England and set up his trust fund with a capital of £150,000. With the interest he built his first flats in Commercial Street, Spitalfields, in 1864. The buildings of the Peabody Fund are always recognizable because of their air of solidity, sobriety and bowdlerized classicism ('horrors', Pevsner has called them). On sites such as that at the back of Victoria Station, Peabody built his flats to accommodate workmen with 'improving' temperaments. Drunkenness was, of course, frowned on and the substantial iron gates which surrounded each Peabody block were locked at midnight to discourage activities conducive to moral decay. To set their standards of plain, solid respectability the architects of the Peabody tenements often chose a chaste version of the 'Queen Anne' style to express best the intentions of the architecture. Peabody's work has continued throughout this century and it has been untouched by the influence of the Modern Movement.

Mansion House flats

These tenements were among the earliest English experiments in flat building. They were created for working-class residents but, at the same time, flats were being designed for a different sort of clientele—the rich. It is one of the more important principles to grasp about flats that they were conceived as economy or utility dwellings both for the rich and the poor. It was only much later

Figure 7 Henry Roberts Model Dwellings for Families, Bloomsbury, 1849, plan

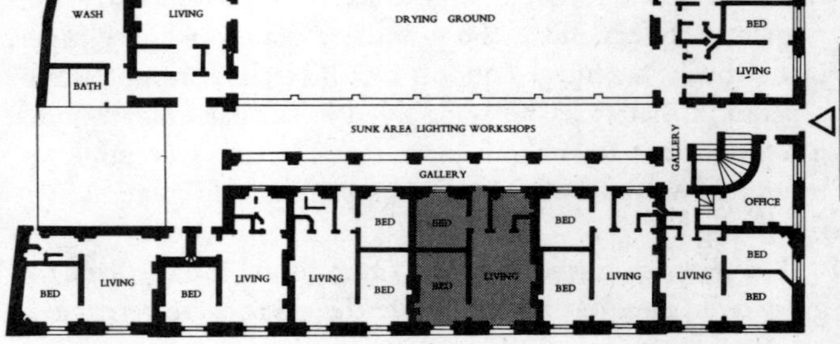

[1] See Vanessa Parker, *The English House in the Nineteenth Century*. London, Historical Association, 1970.
[2] See Nikolaus Pevsner, *London II*, Buildings of England Series, Harmondsworth, 1952, pp. 216, 422–3.

in the twentieth century that it began to be considered desirable, or even likely, that middle-class people should choose to live in purpose-built flats. It was the introduction of the flat as an acceptable type of accommodation for the middle class that was the aim of radical, modernist thinkers like Wells Coates. Naturally, among the class of people who have been least familiar with living in flats there was resistance to change. There was a similar resistance when the building of the tenement blocks began to influence the creation of flats in the mansion house style for the rich. For instance, referring to the tradition of tenement building for the working classes in London, a writer in *The Building News* for 1868 expressed the potential of the type:

> Dwellings in flats are no longer built exclusively for the lower classes. They are being adopted by the other extreme of society . . . we hope before long to see them . . . adopted by the middle strata.
>
> (*Building News* XV, 15 May 1868, p. 323, cited by J. N. Tarn in Anthony Sutcliffe (ed.) *Multi-storey Living*, Croom Helm, 1974, p. 24)

The two types of flat (the tenement and the mansion house) never coalesced into one form before the First World War. It has been only in this century that the principle and form of the English flat has approached establishing itself as a building type. There were, however, prior to this some unusual experiments made before the grouping of flats in a common block became *the* established practice. Among these was the curious 'half-house', rather similar to the Byker flats, built on the Warner and Winn estates in the Pretoria Avenue–Forest Road area of Walthamstow in 1905. This design solution, which existed with variations until the 1930s in areas such as Wembley Park, was to provide individual self-contained accommodation for a family on the ground floor and similar accommodation above while all the time the appearance to the passer-by was of a coherent whole. Access was by either a common street door or, as at Byker, by two doors in tandem.[1] Because of the better insulation from street noise and human circulation the first floor in these half-houses was considered more desirable and the rent was often greater than for the ground floor flat. At Pretoria Road, for instance, the differential in rents was 7s and 6s 6d.

These half-houses, while interesting, are only a diversion for they did not influence the course of development of the flat in England. Rather, the type of flat which was most impressive in establishing an identity for the building type was not the tenement nor the half-house but the luxurious mansion-house type. Established in the later nineteenth and early twentieth centuries it is this sort of flat which most influenced public acceptance of the new mode. 'Mode' is exactly the right word, for it was with the influence of continental fashions in mind that the very earliest propagandists for flat building articulated their argument. This was not, however, without a trace of proto-Functionalist philosophy. A writer in *The Journal of the Society of Arts* wrote in 1876 to satirize the traditional English form of living in multi-storey houses. He said that:

> From the bottom to the top of this house is an open shaft, called the staircase, which is a complete conductor of smell, noise and draught, an intolerable evil to old people, children and invalids.
>
> (T. Roger Smith and W. H. White, 'Model Dwellings for the Rich' in *The Journal of the Society of Arts* XXIV, 31 March 1876, pp. 456 *et seq.* Cited by J. N. Tarn in Sutcliffe, *op. cit.*, p. 20)

Further suggesting the influence of the continent, many of the mansion-house blocks were built in a style that is a variation of Beaux-Arts classicism although many others were built in quite distinctive manners which defy stylistic pigeon-holing. Many, like W. H. Scrymgeour's Bickenhall Mansions of 1896 in Baker Street, (film strip 6) or Reginald Morphew's Marlborough Chambers, Jermyn Street, include riotously disorganized and unergonomic planning arrangements wedded to their bastardized styles. Even architects directly in the tradition of modern architecture, like Richard Norman Shaw, were not free from blame when it came to finding a style of architecture appropriate to a mansion house block. Indeed, to choose Shaw's Albert Hall Mansions (1879), the first mansion house block in London, as an example suggests that even the most talented architects had difficulty in tackling such grand new schemes [**Plate 49**]. Certainly, Shaw's style may have been influential in establishing an identity for the type but the Albert Hall Mansions were never considered an aesthetic success. *The Builder* said of them:

> Of the design the less we say the better, suffice it that an Athenian would not have understood it, a Roman would have called it barbarous, a Goth would have shuddered at it.
>
> (*The Builder*, XXXVI, 12 January 1878, p. 37. Cited by J. N. Tarn in Sutcliffe, *op. cit.*, p. 37)

That outlay or convenience or, indeed, elegance were not considerations to be taken into mind when designing flats for the rich in this period can be proved by a brief discussion of one of the more prominent mansion-house types, Edwin T. Hall's The Mansions, Sloane Gardens Chelsea [**Plate 50**].

It is difficult to describe accurately the style which Hall chose for The Mansions, because on this six-storey building he wedded what can only be called renaissance details to a structure which in its forms and massing can only be called gothic. Admittedly, he had a difficult, segmental site on which to build and, in a way, his design solution matches the site quite well. On one street façade he has three projecting bays while the other is a gently curving arc. The three projecting bays extend to the

[1] See Alan A. Jackson, *Semi-detached London*, Allen & Unwin, 1973.

whole height of the building serving only to emphasize its precipitous height, the effect of which Hall tried to diminish by three massive string courses which embrace the building. Atop the welter of square, segmental, triangular and broken pediments which form the principal decorative features of the façade, Hall stretched a ludicrously dainty little balustrade, utterly out of proportion to the bulk of the building and dwarfed by the enormous square chimneys which serve the fire place in the library, dining room and kitchen. Style was not a criterion nor, it seems, in these flats built for masters and servants, was function.

Hall's flat plan follows the awkward shape of the site. The Mansions employed the most extravagant form of layout for there was only one flat per floor; they were served by a single lift running up the centre of the stairwell. There was a small, square hall feeding into the dining room, drawing room, library and bathroom. The three main bedrooms were fed by an internal corridor leading off the hall. At the end of the corridor, at the farthest possible remove from the dining room, was the kitchen and scullery. Hall's residents evidently did not want cooking smells to upset them while they ate! These service areas, which were, incidentally, served by their own lift, because of their position distant from the dining room, necessitated the food's being carried along the corridor past the bedrooms and through the hall before it arrived at the dining-room table. Sure enough an indication that although no accommodation for a maid is singled out on the plan a maid there must certainly have been.

The drawing room and dining room both had balconies and the curiously shaped site and the exigencies of Hall's chosen plan resulted in there being a dog's leg shaped court running down the centre of the building.

Besides Norman Shaw and Edwin Hall there were many other architects practising in this architectural vein in the late Victorian and early Edwardian eras. Many famous names are associated with the expensive, fashionable flats built around St James's and Hanover Square; E. P. Warren built Hanover House, St James's, and Paul Hoffmann built the flats at No. 14 Hanover Square. Occasionally the same firm of architects would design both luxury mansion-house flats for the rich and slightly more modest flats on the same pattern for the rising professional classes who were less well-to-do. Often, such flats would only be a few streets apart; the firm of Boehmer and Gibbs built both Harley House, Regent's Park, and the less expensive Sandringham Court, Maida Vale. The difference in rentals would be accounted for not necessarily by superior architecture or fittings but, instead, by the tone of the neighbourhood.

Such preposterous buildings do not, of course, have anything to do with the history of the intellectual dissemination of the Modern Movement aesthetic and philosophy in England. They did, however, do much to establish a readily recognizable type of inner city flat building.

So you can see that at the beginning of the century two types of flats were well established: the working man's tenement and the rich man's mansion-house. The taste for flats was yet to spread to the middle classes. Canvassing for the cause of flats was to become the business of the Modern Movement but the seeds of the taste were already forming in the middle-class consciousness. Wider experience of hotels and the increasing availability of popular travel made the *appartement*, *Wohnung* and *Miethaus* familiar terms by 1905, but W. Shaw Sparrow was not optimistic that the developers could win the favours of the middle class:

> If the speculators in flats . . . think that they can win the suffrage of the middle classes, they might as well find investment for their capital by discovering diamond fields in the Isle of Man. They would do well to note that the growing exodus from London into Garden Cities proves beyond doubt that flats have popular rivals to contend against.
>
> (W. Shaw Sparrow, *op. cit.*, p. 18)

We now know this to have been an accurate prophecy, for the lure of a cottage in the country which the Garden City Association offered was irresistible to English taste. But in 1905 the field was wide open for a new development in flats to make an appeal to a broad section of the populace. One of the problems faced by the proponents of the flat was the choosing or creation of a style appropriate to the building. Sparrow thought that architectural style was immaterial to the desirability of the building. He wrote that

> There is one very conspicuous block of flats in London where the exterior is the very negation of architecture, and yet has always been well tenanted.
>
> (W. Shaw Sparrow, *op. cit.*, p. 86)

But you should not be misled into thinking that Sparrow's was a proto-modern theory of functionalism. Rather he was inveighing against a misapplication of historicist styles. He did, however, allow that 'convenience of planning and internal arrangements . . . will attract far more tenants than any external architectural effect'.[1] Quite how novel this thought was can best be demonstrated by a contrast with the theory of the architect Frank T. Verity who wrote in the same publication as Sparrow. Verity's thought shows how little it was considered necessary that a block of flats should clearly articulate its function from without. He thought the mansion-house type should be literally disguised as a large town house: this was the very essence of the mansion-house type of flat building—its very basis on architectural deceit. Needless to say, Verity would have chosen Beaux-Arts classicism as the style best suited to ex-

[1] W. Shaw Sparrow, *op. cit.*, p. 86.

press his grandiose vision. Yet, despite his influence, there were inklings even among the establishment that this historicist icing was doing the cake no good at all. Sparrow lamented that

At a time when England leads the way in decorative design, it is singular that so much creative tawdriness should be admitted into the decoration of flats.

(W. Shaw Sparrow, *op. cit.*, p. 23)

and although his imagined ideal of honest Arts and Crafts flats was never to materialize the First World War marked the abrupt end of this careless and disorganized reign of speculative, historicist flat building.

After the cataclysm the field was open. The combination of state intervention in housing policy and direct influence from the continent was to create the conditions of receptivity to new forms and new ideas. It was at this time that the idea of the third category of flat building, the modern flat, was introduced into England.

2 F. R. S. Yorke and Frederick Gibberd's 'The Modern Flat'

In 1937, when the Architectural Press published Yorke and Gibberd's *The Modern Flat*, the two young men were already well established in the architectural world. Frederick Reginald Stevens Yorke, who died in 1955 as a partner in the influential firm of Yorke, Rosenberg and Mardall, had published in 1934 his book, *The Modern House*, a paean to the International Style, and Frederick Gibberd, who is still a practising and highly respected architect whose most famous work is the Metropolitan Cathedral of Christ the King of Liverpool, had a number of important commissions behind him. Like most young architects in the 1930s these two were captivated by the heady romantic fiction of the International Style (see Appendix). Because both flats and this aesthetic were considered continental imports (and rightly so), a certain identity of values grew up to surround them. The lyricism of Le Corbusier's Apollonian aesthetic and the philosophical rigour of Gropius's functionalism—as marketed through the CIAM (Congrès internationaux d'architecture moderne)—were powerful inducements to Yorke and Gibberd to formulate an approach to domestic building and a style for it that were literally foreign to England. Both men readily adopted the articles of faith of CIAM policy and used *The Modern Flat* as a vehicle for propaganda of their principles.

Section 2 is essentially an edited extract from pp. 19–40 of this book. *The Modern Flat* contains an introduction, analysis of building types and interior arrangements and a fully illustrated 'catalogue' of the stylistically and ideologically pure examples of flat building in Europe in the 1930s. The edited extract from *The Modern Flat* is from the section where Yorke and Gibberd discuss the different types of building (a) and describe the possible interior arrangements (b). The importance of these clear, didactic analyses cannot be overstated. Yorke and Gibberd set out to describe to the receptive reader just what a modern flat was. The very fact that they considered this to be necessary in a specialist publication speaks volumes for the amount of canvassing still needing to be done for the International Style and flats in England in the 1930s. The section on the building types (a) was written with the intention of clearing up the fundamental accessibility problems. Put more simply, this means 'If there is more than one dwelling in a given building, *how do you get at the front door*?' In their discussion of the building types you will see that Yorke and Gibberd swallowed the narrow-minded deceits of CIAM lock, stock and barrel. Their approach was, in any case, uncritical but their enthusiasm for the modernist philosophy made them on occasions dowright irrational. (The stated aims of CIAM are, reprinted in *Form and Function*, Part 4. No. 103.) Their section on interior arrangement, reprinted in edited form as (b), is a little more clear-headed and describes the constraints operating on any architects not only in the design of flats but in the design of any domestic unit. Because of this you should read (b) very carefully. Both apply to flat buildings designed each side of the 1930s and, with the lessons learnt in mind, you should be able to apply Yorke's and Gibberd's external and internal analyses to any flat buildings you see or read about.

a Building types

Corridor Access

Corridor type flats are those to which access is provided by means of internal passages, with flats on one or both sides, fed by staircases or staricases and lifts at convenient points.

The corridor type is the crudest flat plan and is normally the easiest to devise. It is consequently very popular.

The first and obvious disadvantage is that the tenant, having made his vertical ascent by lift, is required to travel some distance horizontally along the building before arriving at the entrance to his apartment.

The corridor type is uneconomical in floor space. To obtain natural ventilation and lighting the rooms of the flat must be side by side, and communication between them by secondary internal corridors. Thus a central access corridor with flats on either side involves the provision of three parallel corridors. The larger the flat the more unsuitable the system, since the rooms become strung out with long internal corridors connecting them.

Corridor flats are hygienically inferior to other types for, since each flat has only one external wall, it is difficult to obtain proper cross-ventilation in the rooms.

A building of the corridor type is expensive to run—there are heavy maintenance items in artificial light, cleaning, and decoration of large unlettable areas. Furthermore, unless special precautions are taken against noise by means of heavy carpets—again expensive to keep clean—and acoustic treatment to walls and ceilings, the corridor may become a sound box, transmitting noise throughout the building.

The corridor type is, however, suitable for one-room or two-room flats, which are similar in character and function to hotel rooms. In such apartments a single room is sub-divided for the various living activities, and no internal hall-corridor is necessary, a small lobby being sufficient to separate the flat from the main access corridor [**Fig 8**].

Figure 8 An internal corridor plan

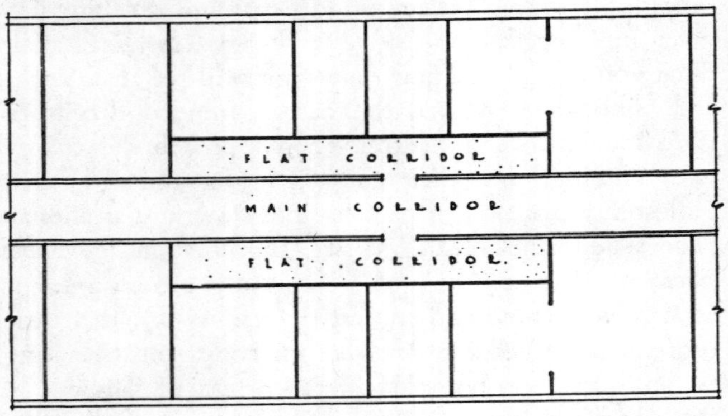

Gallery access

Gallery type flats are those to which access is provided by means of open galleries, fed by staircases, or by staircases and lifts, which may be open or enclosed. The access gallery type building consists in its simplest form of a series of flats, side by side, with an open gallery, usually on the north, connecting them. The gallery, like the corridor plan, may be objected to because it involves traversing the building horizontally, after the vertical ascent has been made. Unlike the corridor, the gallery is open to the air, and in cases where the staircase is enclosed, tenants must go back into the open air again after having entered the building. This disadvantage is, however, more than compensated by the fact that the flat with gallery approach has external walls on its opposite sides, so that rooms can be properly cross-ventilated. An exceptionally simple plan naturally evolves from this one-flat-deep building type, particularly because the open gallery allows natural lighting in two external walls of each flat.

Simplicity in plan shape, simple cross-ventilation, and the ease with which one or two staircases can be made to serve a large number of flats, makes the gallery plan especially popular for low rental flats. In high rental flat planning these advantages are outweighed because, with the gallery open to the air, it is not possible to obtain a sense of luxuriousness from expensive wall and floor coverings, heating and intimate lighting, and such features that induce high rents, and can be obtained in halls or corridors.

In England the access gallery is much used for slum clearance schemes, although it is seldom suitable for this type of work. It is used because the long runs of the galleries enable exceptionally large buildings with hundreds of cross-ventilated flats to be fed by only two or three staircases. This splitting of the cost of the stairs over a large number of flats, and the avoidance of expensive

Figure 9 A gallery access plan

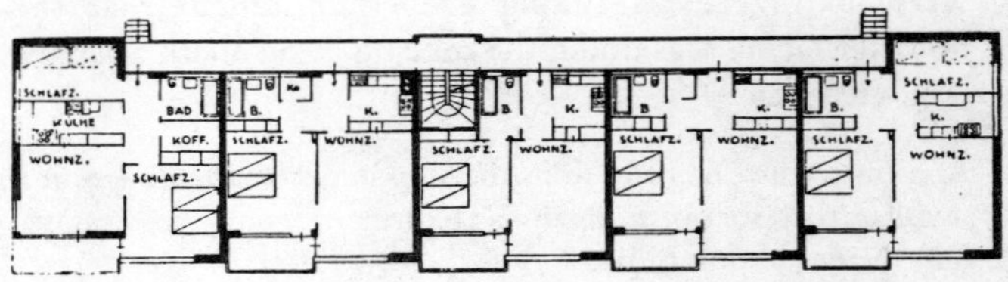

corridors—a gallery requiring only a cheap floor finish and a brick or concrete balustrade— and the structural simplicity of a building only one flat deep, makes for relatively low building costs. But to obtain compact flat plan with more than two or three rooms, it is necessary to make habitable rooms overlook the gallery. These rooms are not fit for sleeping or resting in. A shadow is cast over then from the gallery, and they are overlooked by tenants of other flats who are walking from the staircase to their own homes. Obscure glass does not provide a solution as it obstructs the outlook from the room. Passers-by are close to open windows, so that footfalls, talking and sometimes shouting, make it impossible to get rest and quiet. It has been argued that few people use the gallery at night, and therefore bedrooms may look on to it. This is not reasonable, because the rooms may be used by children who go to bed in the evening, and in any case, workers who start out early may be on the gallery at five or six o'clock in the morning [**Fig 9**].

Direct access

Direct access flats are those entered immediately from halls, fed by staircases, or in tall buildings by staircases and lifts.

With direct approach, once the vertical ascent is made, the tenant is at the entrance door of his home. Furthermore, the means of access occupies only a small amount of floor area, and is economical in landlords' services—heating, lighting and cleaning. Its advantage over the other enclosed access type, the corridor, is that in direct access flats it is possible to provide proper cross-ventilation.

Direct single. The simplest form of direct plan provides one flat per floor per stair. This is an expensive form of building; the cost of the stair and halls can be spread over only a few flats. It becomes more economical if the building is really tall but in districts where height is limited to seven or eight storeys the proposition is seldom reasonable because the lift costs would have to be met by relatively few tenants.

Direct in pairs. Flats planned on either side of a staircase, or lift and staircase. The plan form is a good one, particularly for buildings three storeys high, where a lift is not needed.

Complete cross-ventilation is obtained for each flat, and the building shape is ideal for large open sites where the blocks can be arranged in series, running north and south, to give west light to living rooms on one side and east light to bedrooms on the other.

The London County Council have erected many five-storey buildings on this plan. The two upper floors are arranged as maisonettes so that no tenant is required to climb more than four flights of stairs (though ideally three flights should be a maximum). In Germany the four storey direct in pairs plan has long superseded the gallery type. Owing to lift costs, flats planned direct in pairs are not generally found in medium-rental work in tall buildings, although there are some exceptions; but more expensive flats of this type are common.

Direct Grouped. When three or more flats are grouped round a staircase or lift hall they may be termed direct grouped. Groups have many of the advantages of pairs, and are generally cheaper in cost, particularly if there are four or more flats per floor, as the initial and maintenance costs of means of access can be shared by a considerably larger number of tenants.

They present a more difficult problem in planning because ingenuity is required to give the rooms suitable aspect, to keep the constructional system simple, and to obtain well lighted and ventilated lift and staircase halls in reasonably small space.

The cruciform plan is the most common, and this presents few planning difficulties when the stair and lift can be placed in the dark area in the centre, but building regulations in England require the stairs to open on to the external air, which usually means that the entrance hall must be unduly large.

The problem of lighting the central hall can be overcome when the plan is not regular. North or east aspect for some of the rooms is bound to occur and cross ventilation must be sacrificed when a large number of flats is arranged on all sides of a central hall.

The width of a staircase enclosure should not be less than 7ft. 6 in. to allow ample room for two 3 ft. 6 in. flights.

In the case of three-room or four-room flats which have two or more external walls, the hall, without being long and narrow, can be used to insulate the rooms from one another if it is planned in the heart of the flat, with the rooms grouped around, and having access from it [**Fig 10**].

Figure 10 A plan of a typical group of direct access flats

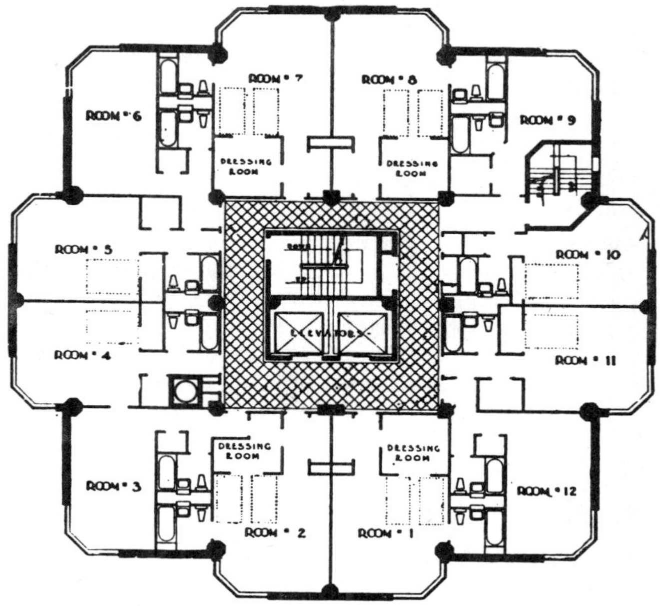

reach was not easy to keep clean, and lighting was normally inadequate. It is now more usual for the doors themselves to be of glass; and a satisfactory arrangement, found often in recent English work, is a pair of double-glazed doors between the hall and living room, which can give adequate lighting in what is usually the darkest part of the flat, and create a feeling of spaciousness through an apparent extension of the living room.

Hall and lobby

When the plan is a long rectangle, the apparent length of the hall may be reduced by forming a lobby at the entrance door end. But with larger flats, or flats with only one external wall where rooms are strung out side by side, the hall is bound to develop into a corridor if it is to serve as a common space to separate all the rooms from one another.

Zone halls

On the other hand, it is not essential that one hall should serve both the living and the sleeping zones; and the long corridor hall can be eliminated by giving each zone its own hall or lobby, and allowing the living space to form the connecting link between them. The American example demonstrates the simplicity of this arrangement; the kitchen, living, dining and maids' rooms have access to a hall at the entrance door end of the plan, and the bedrooms and bathrooms are grouped round a second hall or lobby planned centrally. The living space is crossed only at one end, so that a minimum of disturbance is caused in the room. Under no circumstances should it be necessary to cross the living room diagonally in going from one lobby to another.

Borrowed light

The hall is almost invariably in the heart of the plan, without external walls, so that natural lighting must be borrowed through the rooms. In earlier flats this was done by means of fan-lights over all doors opening on to the hall, but the glass out of arm's

One-room flats

In small one-room and two-room flats difficulties of internal circulation and lighting do not arise because the hall is little more than a lobby for insulating the entrance foor from the living space, and as such is formed by a short length of partition and a curtain.

Dining hall

The average width of the hall in the larger flat is between five and six feet, which is sufficient for receiving and interviewing visitors; and as the length is often more than six feet, some flat planners have thought fit to increase the width, and to use the hall as a dining room. Where this is done the entrance hall must be screened by a lobby, so that callers shall not create undue disturbance; and if it is likely a maid will be employed it is best to provide direct access from the kitchen to this lobby.

There are disadvantages: the dining-hall is a large room to light indirectly, and even when good lighting can be obtained, the smell of cooking is apt to hang about through absence of direct external ventilation.

b Internal arrangements

The amount of time spent in the home has in recent years been much reduced through such innovations as the cinema, cheap travel, playing and watching games, careers for women, creches, and so on; and it is not now so desirable as it was formerly that the dwelling should be large in area, to provide variety in morning room, libray, music room, conservatory, etc. Dining and withdrawing room, sometimes combined as a sub-divided living room, normally suffice. But the same gain in freedom that makes it possible for more time to be spent out of doors, creates for indoor living a definite and increasing demand for light and air, and a feeling of spaciousness.

On the other hand, though the flat may have one or several rooms, it must be relatively small in total area if rent is to be economical.

The organisation of the plan requires much contrivance in exploiting this small space in such a way that it will house all the equipment essential in the modern home, whilst leaving sufficient space for the occupant to expand mentally and physically. There must be no waste space, every inch of it must serve some useful purpose. It may perhaps appear elementary to say there is no place for nooks and crannies, dead angles, corridors and unfurnishable room shapes. But after studying normal speculative flat plans in any country, the remark does not appear superfluous.

The zones

Activities in the dwelling may be classified conveniently under the general headings, living and sleeping—or, day and night.

Living then includes indoor leisure, reading, writing and entertaining, eating and the preparation of food. Sleeping includes dressing, bathing and bed.

The space is therefore planned in two zones; one includes sitting, writing and dining room and kitchen; the other: bedoroms, dressing space, wardrobe and bathroom.

In the two-storey house these zones are isolated on different levels, and there can be no confusion of their elements. But in the plan for the flat, where they are on the same level, the need for consideration of their separate functions often escapes attention.

A first requirement of the flat plan is that the rooms be grouped in two distinct zones, although halls or lobbies may be common to both.

Hall

The main purpose of the hall is to insulate the rooms from the entrance door, and thus from the public parts of the building, and to provide a space where callers may be interviewed in private.

Corridor hall

In early flat plans the hall, in the shape of a long corridor, widened near the entrance door to provide space for the reception of guests, is used to insulate the rooms from one another. Corridors being neither habitable nor workable, are so much waste space, so the plan makes use of them survives only in luxury flats, where the expense of wasted floor area can be reclaimed in high rents.

Living space

Space enough for perfect freedom of movement is more vitally important in the living area than in any other part of the flat. When for economic reasons the size of the flat must be reduced, space in the living room is the last to be sacrificed.

A minimum area for living space in one-room and two-room flats is 140 square feet, and in larger flats, 160 square feet. The average width of the room is between eleven and twelve feet. A minimum dimension of less than eleven feet restricts movement unduly, unless some provision is made for space extension, as at Pullman Court (page 48) where a 14 ft. × 11 ft. living room in a two-room flat is separated from the bedroom by a sliding wall, so that on occasions the whole space can be used as one large room. In a flat housing four or five people, a reasonable living room area is 200 square feet with a minimum dimension of 12 feet.

Elements

The room will be so arranged that the various activities taking place in it can be located, and confusion of its elements avoided. There will be space for sitting, out of cross-draughts, and usually around a source of radiant heat; a space for writing and study near a window, where a desk may have good light and be as much isolated as possible from conversation in the sitting space; a space for shelves and cupboards to house the books and journals that compose the modern library; and a space for dining table and sideboard.

Dining space

The separate dining room that was almost invariably provided in earlier speculative flats has now practically disappeared, having been absorbed in the main living space, which is consequently increased in area to allow the part of it near the kitchen to be set aside as a dining space.

In a small two-room or three-room flat the dining table is usually placed against a wall near the door, so that it is not necessary for food to be carried across the living space. If the table is against the wall between dining space and kitchen, it is usual to form a double-door hatch in the wall so that meals can be served direct from the kitchen on to the dining table.

Dining recess

The main disadvantage of combined dining and living space is that the occupants are aware of the meal to come or the meal past. It is more satisfactory, where a little extra space permits, to provide a dining recess, large enough to accommodate the table, chairs and sideboard, that can be screened before and after meals.

If a door can be arranged between the kitchen and dining recess, preparation and clearing of the dining table in no way interferes with activities in the living space.

The screen between the two parts of the room is, in its simplest form, a curtain hung from a ceiling track. Folding doors give better insulation, but are more expensive and occupy more space. The present-day tendency is to screen the table by a light, free-standing partition, or by a built-in fitment which can serve as a sideboard, with its top only a little above eye level, so that whilst the table is hidden from the living space, the apparent size of the room is not reduced.

Even in those flats where the living space is large enough for the dining room to be planned separately, it should still be possible to throw it into the living room to give a really large space for entertaining.

Kitchen

The reduction to a minimum for space in the kitchen, that must follow when all available space is given to the living rooms, need not be a disadvantage in an area that is rightly considered as a machine for the preparation of meals, and which will operate most efficiently when all equipment is at hand, and no walking from side to side is necessary.

The situation of the kitchen in the flat plan will depend upon the position of the dining space and entrance door, to both of which it must have convenient access. In large flats it may also have access to a service pantry and to a tradesmen's entrance.

Its wall or walls will be, for preference, on north or east. Direct sunlight can make the most well-kept small kitchen unbearably stuffy.

A separate tradesmen's door is particularly desirable where a maid is likely to be in occupation of the kitchen for the greater part of the day, so that interviews with milkmen and butchers' boys do not interfere with the privacy of the flat.

Size

In a small flat the kitchen is generally planned as a narrow rectangle, with entrance door at one end and window at the other. In this form, its equipment can be ranged on one long wall, and the kitchen occupies a minimum of the building frontage. If a kitchen of this type has a width of 4 ft. 6 in. to 5 ft. 6 in. and a length of 8 ft. to 10 ft. the sink may be at the end, under the window, and the cooker, refrigerator and other equipment ranged with the storage units on one long wall. If the width can be increased to 6 ft., the storage units and the equipment can be separated, and ranged on opposite walls. Dimensions across the width would then be: storage units 16 in., working space 36 in., equipment 20 in. An increase in width to 7 ft. would enable equipment to be placed against either wall, giving much greater freedom in planning, and consequently a more efficient working kitchen; and since equipment under the window makes inaccessible angles on either side, it could be omitted. If the kitchen is widened out to a square, as may happen in a large flat, equipment can be placed against any of the four walls. But on the whole, a rectangular kitchen plan is more satisfactory than a square, because with a rectangle it is easier to avoid inaccessible angles.

Economy in building frontage is not so important in kitchens in flats of access gallery type, where one of the long sides of the kitchen is normally on an external wall overlooking the gallery.

Lay-out

The kitchen lay-out is determined by the various jobs that take place in it, the shape and size of the equipment necessary for the work, and the provision of storage space for food and utensils **[Fig 11]**.

The main kitchen tasks are: preparation of food, cooking, serving, dish washing and stacking. The essential equipment includes: cooker, sink with draining board, work-table or other work surfaces, refrigerator and/or larder, storage units for the goods, utensils and cleaning materials. The kitchen equipment is grouped according to the purpose it is to serve; table, cooker, sink, etc., being arranged along the wall to give as nearly as possible a continuous working surface.

The preparation of food takes place on a working surface 2 ft. 6 in. × 1 ft. 8 in., minimum size, located near the food storage units, so that foodstuffs are at hand; at the sink, where vegetables are prepared and near which they should be stored. The serving centre—serving hatch or dresser—becomes a collecting station between the cooker and work table, and the dining table. In large flats it may take the form of a small recess fitted with table and cupboards for dinner and tea services. In the normal flat it is either a storage cupboard near the door, or a battery of cupboards grouped round a hatch between kitchen and dining table. The sink must have good light from a window above or at the left of it, and boards at either side will allow dishes to be stacked, sorted, put through the sink and drained. The stacking and draining board should each be equal in width to the sink, and not less than 2 ft. long. The cupboard for cleaning materials is often fitted in the kitchen near the door leading to the entrance hall, but it may open on to the hall or lobby. Its depth need not be more than 18 in. and its width that of a standard door.

Figure 11 An idealized kitchen

In low-rental flats, space must be provided for a wash boiler. In higher-rental flats, where linen will be sent to an outside laundry, it is still advisable to provide a folding ironing board, which can be built in as a panel of the cleaning cupboard door. An unpleasant practice that still persists in certain low-rental flats is the combined kitchen and bathroom. The inconvenience it produces cannot be justified by the small initial outlay such arrangement will effect.

Bathrooms

In a small flat the bathroom may be approached from the main hall, where its door should be next to those of the bedrooms. In larger flats, where it is necessary to cross the living room to reach the sleeping zone, a small lobby is needed to keep the bathroom apart from the bedrooms and the living space. Under no circumstances should a bathroom open directly from the living room; or when it contains a w.c., from a bedroom. A normal method of isolating the bathroom is to arrange it between two bedrooms, so that a lobby is automatically formed, because a bathroom can be at least 3 ft. less in length than the bedrooms.

In low-rental flats the bathroom is almost invariably planned back to back with the kitchen, in order that plumbing and other services may be grouped in a vertical duct, and have branches of minimum length. Whilst this arrangement is economical in first cost, it may easily cause confusion between living and sleeping zones. Back-to-back kitchen and bathroom planning occurs often in recent London work, in two-room corridor-type flats; kitchen and bathroom being planned between living room and bedroom, so that the plan falls naturally into the two zones.

Apart from the simplification of plumbing and services thus obtained, further economies follow, because the flat can be planned in three equal bays, to give a standardised unit spacing for members of the structural frame.

Astonishing plans have resulted from the dovetailing of equipment on the wall between kitchen and bathroom, in the attempt to reduce building frontage by reducing the overall dimension of the two rooms when they are planned alongside. A popular device is to treat the bathroom as a passage, 3 ft. wide, with the W.C. at one end under the window, and the bath and basin in a recess projecting into the kitchen. This ingenuity is somewhat misplaced; it may enable an extra flat to be crammed on to the site, but it cannot give a sufficient space for bathing.

Two-room flats that are approached by an access gallery, may have their bathrooms behind the bedrooms and overlooking the gallery. This gives a cross ventilated flat with good internal lay-out, and with economical arrangement and services, because the bathroom in one flat can share a vertical duct with the kitchen in the flat adjoining it.

In flats that have two bathrooms, one will be for general use and the other either for the domestic staff or as a private bathroom for the owner. A maid's bathroom will normally have a W.C., and will be planned *en suite* with her bedroom. The owner's bathroom will probably be entered from the main bedroom via a dressing room, the W.C. being separate.

Size and lay-out

The minimum-frontage long-and-narrow bathroom, with door at one end and window at the other, is the most common type in English flat plans; the W.C. is at the window end, the bath against one long wall, and the basin on the same wall nearer the door.

The W.C. is placed under the window for convenience in connecting to a main waste pipe running down the external wall. Where local bye-laws allow the pipes to be arranged in a duct within the building, the positions of W.C. and lavatory basin can, with advantage, be transposed. The W.C. will then be screened when the door is open and the basin will have better natural lighting. This passage shape for the bathroom is not ideal, and a great improvement is made when the width of the room can be increased sufficiently to allow the bath to be placed under the window, to give a more square shape to the free floor space. If it is possible for the room to be entered from the side, the arrangement can be still further improved by placing the bath against the wall opposite the window, where there can be no risk of a bather slipping and putting a hand through the window glass.

When the bathroom is planned next to the kitchen, a double wall between the rooms can be arranged to form a duct about 9 in.

Figure 12 Lubetkin and Tecton, Highpoint, I Highgate, 1935, bathroom

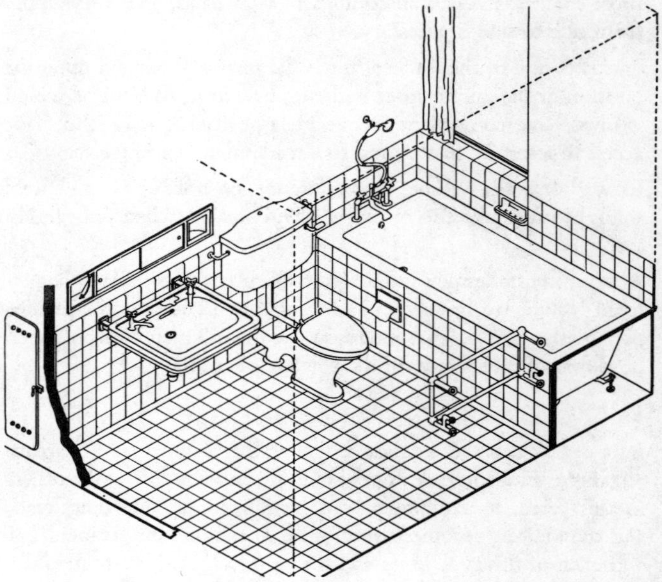

wide. The W.C., lavatory basin and the bath can then be placed against this wall, and the separate pipe branches run direct into the main pipes in the duct. One of the best, but not the least expensive arrangements is to make the bathroom width at least 6 ft. and the depth equal to the length of the bath, plus a pipe duct; with the duct at the end of the bath and the lavatory basin and W.C. at right angles to it. In this way there will be ample space in front of, and between the fittings, although the floor area is not unduly large.

To plan the equipment on three sides of the room is clearly uneconomical, since the service pipes to and from the fittings must then travel round three walls.

Bathroom equipment should include; soiled-linen cupboard, below the basin or in a container housed in the wall; mirror above the basin, and a toilet cabinet either built in behind the mirror or placed to one side of it [**Fig 12**].

1 What is the model of the ideal modern flat suggested by Yorke and Gibberd?

2 Do you have any observations to make on Yorke and Gibberd's analysis of the flat type, its derivatives and internal arrangements? For instance, did you notice any fallacies or intentional deceits?

● 1 Yorke and Gibberd do not actually state their own preference of building type and internal arrangement but their ideal flat block would perhaps be a tall, direct grouped building of more than six storeys, served by lifts, and enjoying fine views. If money were limited then a typical flat plan would have a large living-dining room with a balcony large enough to hold a dining table; a small kitchen with fitted cupboards and a tiled bathroom with hidden pipes. The bedroom(s) would open off the hall. At least two walls of the flat would be exposed to the open air and central heating would enable the provision of large windows.

2 Throughout this passage Yorke and Gibberd chase a number of architectural chimaera: Their obvious obsession with ventilation and hygiene is both a legacy of nineteenth-century conditions and a consistent interest among the architectural avant-garde of the twentieth century (remember Dr Lovell and his American 'Health Houses'). The attention which Yorke and Gibbered give to the ideal of cross-ventilation shows that they were unaware of the possibilities of air-conditioning.

In their anxiety to campaign for the favoured building types of the International Style, the gallery access and the direct access blocks (**Plates 55–56** show the galleries on Wells Coates's Isokon Flats, Hampstead, 1934) they ignored rationality in favour of the plastic opportunities which the sculptural forms of the galleries provide, although they would not have admitted this! It is clear that whether a flat block is corridor, gallery or direct access the resident has to travel the same horizontal and vertical distance from one given point to another given point and no one type has an ergonomic advantage.

In the northern hemisphere windows which face north receive no sunshine. It is an aspect of Yorke and Gibberd's concern for health that they were anxious to ensure direct sunshine for all their rooms. This is ideal in principle but impossible in practice. They appear to be unaware of this.

When Yorke and Gibberd campaign for the small kitchen they betray their debt to Le Corbusier when they call this room a 'machine for the preparation of food' and, at the same time, offer a false example for their illustration. The kitchens at Wells Coates's Isokon flats were only made so small because residents were expected to dine in the Isobar at the bottom of the building. [**Plate 58**]

There is a similar fallacy with the question of servicing. Yorke and Gibberd recommend cutting down space from the kitchen rather than the living room if any economies are desired. This, again, overlooks the fact that in flats for the working-classes the kitchen is the centre of the manual servicing operations. A writer in *The Times* in 1935 acknowledged that an 'immense amount' of labour was required to clean and run the average flat.[1] This labour included washing dirty linen and, for a family who could not afford to patronize a commercial laundry, the kitchen had to become a washroom. The emphasis which Yorke and Gibberd put on the living area betrays their concern with middle-class values. Both appeared to be unaware of the mundane requirements of servicing in working-class flats. Indeed, throughout the edited passage there is a conflict of purpose. The authors do not appear to have their audience clearly in mind; were the flats they were describing intended as solutions to the housing crisis or were they to be merely fashionable new abodes for an educated middle-class which could afford to buy its way out of the difficulties and restraints of flat life?

Despite these fallacies Yorke's and Gibberd's *The Modern Flat* is an engrossing book and it was influential in creating a taste. Their analysis, although it was influenced by the International Style, stands for all time and applies to all kinds of flats. Their book, as its very title suggests, neatly describes the style, ideals and arrangements of that third category of flats, the *modern* flat.

Yorke and Gibberd's attitude to flat design, besides embodying and fundamentally new attitude to housing also encompassed a new aesthetic attitude to architecture's principal constitutents, space and height. ●

Yorke and Gibberd's attitude to space and height

I have taken it as a commonplace that in the minds of 'advanced' architects of the 1930s the cause of flat building and the politico-stylistic intentions of the International Style were treated as an identity. (The reasons for this are suggested later in this Unit, and on this matter you should also consult Anthony Jackson's *Politics and Architecture* (recommended reading.) However, there were, of course, other influences operating besides the philosophical ones—the aesthetic ones. The International Style achieved two fundamental liberations from architectural tradition—the free treatment of space and height. Yorke and Gibberd are more or less aware of these factors throughout their book and both are persistent under-currents in their argument.

Space Any architect practising in the 1930s would have all around him the remains and consequences of nineteenth-century laissez-faire planning: the smelly courts of Victorian tenement blocks, cramped for space and harbours for damp and disease must have contrasted sharply with the persuasive arguments and ivory buildings of Le Corbusier. In an effort to cram as much into as small a site as possible the Victorian developers had created nightmares of claustrophobia. In contrast to this, Le Corbusier's system of construction offered a liberation from the restraints of structural walls. He made vertical planes free. The sense of free space was felt in all dimensions:

> The same gain in freedom that makes it possible for more time to be spent out of doors, creates for indoor living a definite and increasing demand for light and air, and a feeling of spaciousness. (Yorke and Gibberd, *op. cit.*, p. 29)

was how Yorke and Gibberd expressed the feeling. The same feeling of liberation from constraints was carried over into the larger issues of the building's plan. **Plate 51**

[1] James Tudor Craig 'Labour Saved: less home drudgery; kitchen magic'. *The Times*, 3 May 1935, p. xxv.

shows a high-rental block of late Victorian flats built around an enclosed court. Because the developers were anxious to use up all the available frontage the building is planned on the square format and, in feeble deference to the necessity for cross-ventilation, the courts are left as totally wasted area in the centres of the plan.

Plate 52 represents a totally different concept of flat planning. This is a plan of Lubetkin and Tecton's Highpoint I, Highgate, of 1934 (see Units 17–18). The plan is opened out and conceived as a formal whole; six out of eight flats on each floor have daylight and fresh air on three sides. Because of the open plan each room can be uniform and rationally planned. The same sense of spaciousness and absence of useless interruption of interior spaces was made possible both by the new aesthetic and by the new constructional methods which were available by the 1930s.

So much and so often has a new conception of space been hailed as the most important single determinant of the appearance of modern architecture that it is possible to overlook the fact that this feeling of spaciousness found its expression also in the fittings, furnishing and layout of the individual rooms. Wells Coates caught this feeling exactly when, in an article written in 1932, he illustrated the same room in one photograph decorated in a Victorian idiom and in the other in an airy 1930s manner [**Plate 53**]. Yorke and Gibberd used an interior view of Gibberd's own Ellington Court to illustrate their own ideas on interior spatial arrangements [**Plate 54** and film strip 7].

Height The other undercurrent running through Yorke's and Gibberd's book is that of the modern predilection for building high. This, like space, was a function of constructional (and servicing) innovations. Just as their attitude to space was affected by Victorian squalor their attitude to height was similarly moulded by the restrictions of *The London Building Act*. This legislation was framed to prevent the creation of the Victorian slum courts, and one of its strictures was that no building (except churches) should be more than eighty feet tall. This was framed to avoid profiteering by overcrowding and the exclusion of light from narrow streets. In this it was mostly successful but it was, of course, quite contrary to the spirit of Le Corbusier and Gropius who, unhampered by such tight building regulations, were free to theorize about the advantages of high-rise.

Yorke and Gibberd were very conscious of the restraints put upon them by *The London Building Act*; they wrote that 'it is not the *height* of buildings that produces bad conditions; it is the space between them that matters',[1] and so much were they inspired by this restraint that they conceived of high building as the solution to all architectural and socially related problems. According to them a high building gave better views, more light, more fresh air and was cheaper to build. High-rise is now discredited, but these aspiration were an honourable dream in the 1930s.

Indeed, in the praise of the skyscraper flat the International Style functionalists meet the Garden City utopians half way. Following Le Corbusier, projects for tall flat blocks were not illustrated in architect's impressions in urban surroundings (where they were needed) but in verdant countryside like W. A. Eden's project [**Figure 21**]. Anything would look fine in a beautiful setting but so intoxicated were Yorke and Gibberd by the modern dream of sleek tall, concrete and glass blocks going up in parkland across the country that they let go of their rationality. They illustrated a project by the American architect, Raymond Hood, for a twenty-storey tower block in the country. It looked magnificent but the architect conveniently neglected to include in his utopian impression the necessary service facilities: there were no roads, sewage facilities, refuse dumps, smoke-stacks, fuel stores, car parks, bus stops nor any other external services which a working unit demands. The constraints of reality were not, it seems, allowed to stand in the way of the noble vision of heroic tower blocks standing proud, lonely and erect across the countryside.

3 Post First World War legislation and the creation of the local authority tenement in London

In the course of the twentieth century the development of the flat has been matured and refined from its three strains into two, both of which are a division of the *modern flat* type. Firstly, there is the working-class modern flat, built by local authorities and private housing trusts, and secondly there is the professional man's modern flat, built mostly as speculative developments by private builders. This part deals with the early evolution of the working-class modern flat at the beginning of this century. Unlike the speculative builder, local authorities have to respond directly to *needs*, not the whimsies of taste. Therefore the housing which they created gives us a valuable model of the real abilities of modern architecture and planning to find an economical solution to the housing shortage.

Local authority housing is so much an everyday sight of modern life that it is only with an effort of imagination that we can appreciate that it is largely a phenomenon restricted to our century. Victorian legislation, in particular *The Labouring Classes Lodging Houses Act* (1851) and *The Housing of the Working Classes Act* (1890), had invested in local authorities the power—if not the will—to create their own sanitary, modern housing for working people. There were freak exceptions, like the 'cottages' built at Everton in 1869, but generally it is to London, with its tradition of philanthropic housing programmes under-

[1] Yorke and Gibberd, *op. cit.*, p. 20.

taken by, for instance, the Peabody and Guinness trusts, that we must look to see the major initiatives of local authority housing. It is hardly surprising, bearing in mind the size of the city's housing problem and the resources available to solve it, that it was the London County Council and its predecessor, the Metropolitan Board of Works, which carried out the most ambitious schemes of flat building seen in the early part of this century.

The type of housing that the Metropolitan Board of Works was creating in the 1890s was a tenement of four-storey, flat-roofed buildings which had made only little essential progress in either form or convenience from buildings such as those erected by the Birkenhead Dock Company or the flats of *The Society for Improving the Conditions of the Labouring Classes* in Bloomsbury [**Plates 47–48**] in the 1840s.

Crude as the Board of Works' flats might have been, the type illustrated in **Figure 13** represented a temporary peak, for economic conditions were to force the standards of accommodation to decline in the years leading up to the First World War. Typically, a late nineteenth-century flat would be laid out with access by the direct-in-pairs method. The rent charged for a dwelling such as the stereotype 'Plan No. 61' was at the rate of 1s 1d per cubic foot per year. A rent such as this, charged on the basis of space occupied, had the obvious effect of encouraging cramped accommodation.

'Plan 61' was simple, with little provision for privacy because the flat accommodation contained only the most basic necessities (one or two bedrooms, living-room, scullery and wc). The kitchen was a communal one. This plan was improved in 1893 by the addition of a balcony to ease the claustrophobia, but under pressure of necessary economics, the modest spatial luxury of having two flats to each stair was thrown out of the window in favour of four, with a consequent diminution of space.

Plans of tenements designed in 1895 show no individual plumbing to rooms, making them simply unserviced cupboards for human beings; the lavatories were communal lock-ups and the communal sculleries were situated in the corridors. This reduction in servicing (compensated, to an extent, by the provision of a communal laundry) enabled the L.C.C. to reduce the rent to the rate of 9d. per cubic foot per year.

Soon, however, the laundry was beginning to be discredited because it was said that the 'women, when at the tub, corrupted one another and caused trouble'[1] and the communal idea was abandoned. (It is interesting to note that the problem of laundering in flats had been a persistent thorn in the side of idealism: either elaborate and expensive capital plant is required or the provision of adequate space demanded—neither are, of course, possible in low-rental properties. The problem had not been solved as late as the 1930s when the habit of drying

Figure 13 Metropolitan Board of Works, tenement plan No. 61

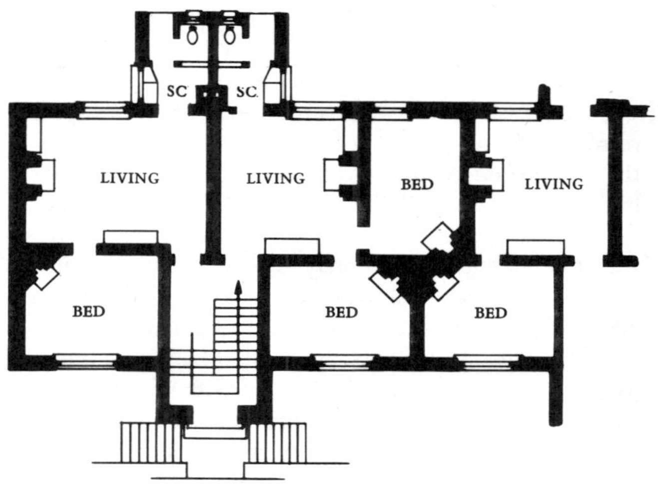

clothes in flats was cited as a major cause of the scourge of rheumatism, and the idea was floated of using the attics of flat blocks, where the heat collected, for clothes drying.) A new direction was found in 1898 when W. E. Riley, the new supervising architect, was appointed. Under Riley, the LCC's flat-building programme began to gravitate towards the gallery access type which later became the staple form of London's local authority flats. W. E. Riley (who was, incidentally, the architect who built the Central School of Arts and Crafts), did much to make the working-class flat an acceptable form of accommodation.

Thus, it was in the first two decades of the new century that we can observe the popular concerns of the modern flat theory emerging in the policy of the LCC but without, at this time, any question of continental influence.

What do you imagine were these new concerns?

• Perhaps as a direct legacy of the slum conditions of early tenements the new twentieth-century flats put emphasis on *space* both in individual accommodation and for communal recreation. Privacy was also to be enhanced by the provision of access galleries which did not interfere with bedrooms, and the economies made by building up to five storeys tall were to be ploughed back into the building. •

The Tabard Street Estate

The Tabard Street Estate [**Plate 59**] was one of the earliest schemes to embody the elements of the new consciousness inspired by Riley. It was rebuilt in 1917 on a 16½-acre site to replace a mid-nineteenth-century slum of two-storey houses crammed on to the site at the rate of eighty to the acre (twelve houses to the acre is a

[1] Wornum, *op. cit.*, p. 439.

'good' figure) and, by building high, the new housing managed to accommodate half the former population with 5 acres left over for recreation. The new flats in fact housed 4,500 people and each family had a living room of at least 160 square feet, and the minimum size of the bedrooms was 100 square feet. The economies of space—giving recreational area which would have been unheard of in the nineteenth-century—were created by building as high as *The London Building Act* would allow. Because of its height, the Tabard Street Estate required lifts. Staircases and lifts, which are extremely expensive to build, in the first case, and buy and maintain, in the second case, have been the economic bugbears of the build-high school since its inception. At Tabard Street the LCC encountered some of the usual difficulties associated with lifts. To prevent vandalism, a scheme was tried where each individual tenant was able to unlock the lift when he required to use it in order to save on the wages of a paid attendant, but because this system made life exhausting and awkward for milkman and visitor alike, who were forced to climb the stairs, it was soon abandoned.

The pattern established by the LCC at the Tabard Street Estate was continued at the East Hill Estate in Wandsworth [**Plate 60**] where the LCC's new chief architect, G. Topham Forrest, decided to build five storeys tall. His mammoth scheme produced impressively fine buildings of heroic dimensions and because of the apparent economies of tall building Forrest felt able to indulge himself and his residents with the addition of decorative details like gauged brick arches which, it was calculated, added only 1d. a year to the rents.

Economy of space was the greatest concern at East Hill and here Forest achieved a density of sixty-six flats to the acre, allowing two people to every habitable room. Although this figure would nowadays be unacceptable, Forrest also included some humane features in his grand architecture and in each internal court he ensured that the darkest corners were given to the communal staircases rather than the individual balconies. The East Hill Estate was given warm critical response, even encouraging the cottage traditionalist, G. Grey Wornum, to advocate quite passionately the ideal of tall building as a source of hope in the solution of the housing shortage.

> Such is the difference in result between two-storey and five-storey building

he wrote, that

> new slums are not created by these modern tenement blocks.
>
> (G. Grey Wornum, *op. cit.*, p. 437)

There was another factor, however, impinging on the creation of the modern local authority flat. This was the chain of legislation which followed the increasing self-awareness on the part of local authorities of their responsibility in the housing problem. The assumption by government that legislation should be framed to help mould the shape and set the standards of housing was to have a profound effect on the development of the flat in England.

Legislation

You will already have read in Unit 20 of the movement immediately after the First World War to provide 'Homes for Heroes'; similarly, you will have seen illustrations of houses built for Woolwich munitions workers. The moving force which went towards solving the crisis in post-war housing which preceded all the major legislation was the so-called Tudor Walters Report. *The Times* reported on 30 January 1918 that the Local Government Board had issued a memorandum to local authorities concerning the pattern of working-class homes. This was, in effect, the Tudor Walters Report, named after its protagonist, the government minister Sir J. Tudor Walters. The Report laid down the minimum desirable conditions for modest housing—ones which we would now regard as obvious but which were by no means established criteria in 1918. The provisions of the Report were both progressive and unexpected and in maintaining that working-class housing should be in the form of single-family dwellings built at a density of twelve to the acre it did much to harden English taste for the cottage home and materially disadvantaged the cause of the flat in this country. The report is important to us in this unit because it set the keynote for government intervention in housing standards and housing policy.

Each Tudor Walters house was expected to last for sixty years and was to have the conventional picturesque apparatus of a small front garden and 'to avoid a monotonous and depressing appearance the number of houses in a continuous row was not to exceed eight or ten'.[1]

Although the Tudor Walters Report predicted the internal conditions of the flats of the 1930s with its specified requirement that there should be a 'sunny aspect for the living room, the bath on the ground floor . . . a store for food and one for fuel',[2] it was very much responsible for the institutional inertia vis-à-vis flats when it declared that 'the erection of blocks of buildings containing a series of tenements should be avoided'.[3] 'Tenement' was the derogatory term used by all opponents of flat building.

The impetus for local authorities, particularly the LCC, to build flats had been provided by the crisis in housing in the immediate post-war period. The crisis was not so much caused by war damage, which was very slight in England and only at all serious in France, but rather by the four-year postponement of all building activity caused by the war. This, and the rapidly rising costs of labour, land and material, forced local authorities to consider the economic benefits of flats (at least as they were then perceived) and encouraged government, by means of

[1] *The Times*, 30 January 1918, p. 9e.
[2] *The Times, loc cit.*
[3] *Ibid.*

extension of credit and making concessions to private housing associations, intervene in the hitherto almost wholly private building sector and introduce legislation which, while not directly encouraging local authorities to build flats, at least emphasized the economic advantages of so doing.

The four fundamental housing acts were passed by Addison in 1919; by Chamberlain in 1923; by Wheatley in 1924 and by Greenwood in 1930. These, together with the 1936 Housing Act, whereby the state agreed to subsidize by up to 75% all building enterprises which followed certain regulations regarding distribution and hygiene, were the most important laws effecting the development of housing policy in England.

THE HOUSING AND TOWN PLANNING ACT, 1919

This act, passed by Addison, saw the beginning of government moves to increase the supply of working-class housing. Previously, this had largely been the province of private companies; manufacturers who built their own model housing and charitable trusts. The law met with sharp reaction from the Conservative benches where it was thought that the housing shortage could soon be satisfied by private enterprise (which had, hitherto, hardly ever found this type of building a profitable venture) and was solely a product of wartime conditions rather than a reflection of weaknesses in the system.

The Addison Act imposed upon local authorities the duty of surveying the need for working-class housing and of making provisions to satisfy it. Before this, local authorities had never been so powerful in housing affairs. Up to March 1927 rents were to be fixed independently of costs. This careless gesture was, of course, calculated to undermine the position of private enterprise in working-class housing for if the government was prepared to underwrite all losses on rents then private enterprise, which by its very nature could not, would appear to be discredited. However, with the Treasury accepting responsibility for losses made by local authorities there was always the danger of temptation to extravagance:

> The subsidy . . . by relieving local authorities of practically all financial responsibility for their housing schemes, created conditions financially highly favourable to a policy of providing houses to let at rents within the reach of those families most in need of houses. . . . At the same time the need for providing a substitute for the financial incentive to economy by means of a purely administrative control of the activities of local authorities, created administrative problems.

(Marion Bowley, *Housing and the State 1919–1944*. Allen & Unwin, 1945, p. 35)

The subsidy, besides encouraging recklessness in spending by the local authorities, also had an inflationary effect in that it created wealth which was more apparent than real.

A new Conservative government elected in 1922 soon brought in new legislation in the form of Neville Chamberlain's *Housing Act* of 1923.

THE HOUSING ACT, 1923

This bill was passed in July 1923 in an attempt to compensate for the excesses perpetrated under the 1919 Act. Chamberlain's act gave equal encouragement to both public and private enterprise by offering subsidies of £6 per house over a twenty-year period whether it was built by a speculative builder or by a local authority. Local authorities were empowered to advance money to prospective residents and the subsidy was seen only as a temporary measure until equilibrium was attained and the rates were not expected to support the expense. It was Chamberlain's intention that the act should encourage owner-occupation and discourage the institution of housing as a social service. Although his intentions were kind, his calculations were based on the assumption that the housing shortage was only a temporary one. Because Chamberlain's act tended to harm the interests of the less well-off family by effectively reducing its chances of getting state or private housing the new Labour government of 1924 soon introduced counter measures.

HOUSING ACT, 1924

The 1924 Housing Act was introduced by Wheatley, the Labour Minister of Health. This act maintained the subsidy introduced by Chamberlain but reinforced the position of the local authorities in the provision of working-class housing by incorporating them as a permanent part of the institutional housing machinery. No government has dared to alter this by subsequent legislation and, although the power of local authorities to provide housing had existed since 1951, it was the Wheatley Act of 1924 which created the real power of 'councils' to provide working-class housing.

Wheatley not only did this but also extended Chamberlain's 1927 subsidy to 1939 and made his famous 'gentleman's agreement' with the building-trade unions. The unions were encouraged to relax their restrictive rules so that more skilled men could be employed; to do this Wheatley employed a circular argument suggesting that the more skilled men the building industry had available the more houses would be able to be built thereby providing more accommodation for working men. It was projected that the amount of houses built should rise from

63–95 thousand in 1926, to
150–225 thousand in 1935.

Greenwood, the second Labour Minister of Health in the government of 1930–1 introduced the most crucial legislation to effect the shape of our cities in 1930, the Slum Clearance Act.

THE SLUM CLEARANCE ACT, 1930

This was the act drawn up to provide for those people who were too poor to be helped by the earlier housing legislation and it was the most potent single influence on the form of our modern cities and the working-class flats which form the subject of part of section 7 of this unit.

Greenwood introduced a system of differential rents and this influential act was passed in an atmosphere of disdain for those who, at least in the imagination of the Labour government, considered aesthetic reward an adequate compensation for poor living conditions. It was against this sort of background that pressure for adequate housing for the working classes was so strong as to disregard the niceties of architecture, and you should bear it in mind when considering the housing schemes which are subsequently discussed in this unit.

Marion Bowley pointed out in 1945 that:

> The fashionable denigration of modern jerry building and the enthusiasm for genuine Tudor and Georgian houses must not be allowed to obscure the implications of this [Greenwood's] Act. Apart from the fact that architectural gems are often most inconvenient to live in, the majority of houses fail most lamentably to provide aesthetic pleasures in compensation for their inherent lack of convenience and comfort.
>
> (Marion Bowley, *op. cit.*, p. 50)

The gem of LCC flat building, the Ossulston Estate in St Pancras, did, however, manage to combine aesthetic satisfaction with convenience and comfort. This estate was planned with the sole object in mind of overcoming the overcrowding in central London, which had also been the target of the 1930 legislation.

The need for high density housing

In the first four decades of this century there was not so much a numerical increase in population as a change in its organization: the three-generations-under-one-roof Victorian family was, in the 1930s, beginning to separate out. These figures speak for themselves:

	Av. family	Families per 1,000 pop.
1901	4.62	216.5
1931	3.91	255.75

(H. Ingham Ashworth, *Flats—Design and Equipment*, Pitman, 1936)

In 1931 the 'terrible overcrowding' meant in real terms that there were 834,000 more families than there were places for them to live. Both the building industry and architects were unable immediately to do anything to solve the problem. At this time, British architectural sociology tended towards rather vague generalizations such as 'the English people dislike the herd life',[1] cited as an argument against the provision of local authority tenements, and lacked the precision of a science. At the same time, however, writers like H. Ingham Ashworth were also acutely aware of the political dangers inherent in a dissatisfied working class and with the Austrian workers' insurrection of 1934 in mind when the Viennese flats were turned into fortresses, Ashworth wrote:

> To gather together masses of people having the maximum reason for discontent and despair would appear to be the very way to foster extreme political movements.
>
> (H. Ingham Ashworth, *op. cit.*, p. 122)

Because of this it was only with the most extreme reluctance that middle-class conservatives could recommend the building of tenement flats but this, of course, was the solution to the housing problem adopted by many local authorities (in particular by London) and you should not forget that the decision to build tenement flats was of an unavoidably political character. Some of the LCC estates were built under the more or less direct influence of continental models, but for the moment, it suits our purpose to treat them as insular schemes.

Certainly, in formalistic and propagandist achievements the Austrians, Germans and Dutch often outpaced the British example but contemporary commentators always considered that British flat development, of which in its early phases the LCC provides the most suitable microcosm, far surpassed its European rivals in the levels of creature comfort attained, in standards of finish achieved and in the sanity of its individual planning.

In London, this was all achieved under pressures greater than those known on the continent. The capital city's vast population was both the cause of its slum problem and an aggravation to the difficulty of temporary rehousing while new developments were under way. A further problem experienced by the LCC was people's resistance to living in flats, for in London, as opposed to, say, Vienna or Berlin, no long tradition of flat-dwelling existed and such as there was for poor people always carried the unpleasant associations of poverty, charity and philanthropy.

Ossulston Estate, St Pancras

It was under the influence of the sublime proportions of the overcrowding in the Euston area G. Topham Forrest and E. Haden Parkes created the Ossulston Estate in St Pancras [**Plates 61–65**], the single most impressive LCC tenement scheme where the new type of architecture for the first time found a style of its own. Both the style and the type of building were created under the influence,

[1] H. Ingham Ashworth, *op. cit.*, p. 121.

more or less direct, of contemporary continental models and Grey Wornum was even moved to remark that Ossulston Street looked like Vienna in London.[1] The original plan for the Ossulston Estate had been for nine-storey blocks which would have necessitated the inclusion of lifts *ab initio* for, as Yorke and Gibberd pointed out, it has always been customary for lifts to be provided in all dwellings of more than three storeys while the more heartless Europeans, particularly the Viennese, were able to realize ambitiously tall schemes at economical expense because they were prepared to make residents walk up to six-storey-high flats. The nine-storey project for the Ossulston Estate became too costly to be executed for it was estimated that a lift there would cost £211 p.a. with the extra expense of £150 p.a. for the attendant's wages.

The final form of the massive Ossulston Street Estate was of four- and five-storey blocks, with one storey hidden in the roof. The architects, doubtless influenced by the propagandist forms of the Viennese flats erected under that city's socialist administration allowed themselves some dalliance with formalism and introduced decorative arcading and segmentally bulging balconies [**Plates 63** and **64**]. Their doorways too gave a positive, if chilling, identity to the whole scheme [**Plate 65**] but their decision to copy the Viennese cement rendering was not a successful one, for the dirty air of Euston station soon stained the buildings and reduced the impact of their effect from heroic grandeur to that of grimy pastry. Although the original nine-storey scheme for the Ossulston Estate was never realized, it, or its four-five-storey realization, may have been the direct inspiration of another unexecuted but highly ambitious rehousing scheme for Limehouse devised by the architects Barnes and Davidge.

The success of these LCC projects has to be judged not only in terms of grandeur of concept but also in comparison with the precedent set by the LCC and its predecessor, the Metropolitan Board of Works.

However commonplace the LCC tenements may immediately appear to modern eyes they, in fact, provided a revolution in hygiene, sanitation and servicing in comparison to their antecedents. A flat designed by G. Topham Forrest for the LCC in 1930 would contain not only the basic living quarters but a long, airy balcony, a private gas copper, a gas cooker, a private WC and a private bathroom. Modest enough luxuries, perhaps, but these LCC tenements if not too daring in style were the representative triumphs of modern architecture's approach to urban housing in Britain in this period. They provided a fully-serviced home where before there had been sooty gas lamps and streaming, dark unlit halls and stairways. The quality of this achievement was not rivalled anywhere on the continent nor, paradoxically, was it aided by new structural techniques.

[1] G. Grey Wornum 'Modern Flats', *Journal of the R.I.B.A.*, 1931, pp. 435–55.

Part two The influence of the continental avant-garde in England

1 Structural and service innovations in building in the 1930s.

Three things affected the shape of flats in the twentieth century. They were different in character, the first being a change in attitude and the last two being dependent on technology.

The first change was the new conception of tall building. As we have seen at the Ossulston Estate the apparent economies achieved by tall building (made possible by new legislation) were used to offset the cost of introducing conventional, but hitherto impossibly expensive, services into each individual flat.

Second was the development of new services. The function which basic services perform in any given building will always be the same: air and water need to be heated, food has to be prepared, washing has to be done and waste has to be disposed of. These are not problems in simple rural cottages but in a massive superblock radical planning and financial undertakings necessitate the careful consideration of each individual service's scope. A coal fire and coal-fired range are more feasible in a cottage where the coal does not have to be carried up four flights of stairs; and, being exposed to fresh air on all sides, drying clothes in a cottage presents none of the problems that it does on the flat. The detailed description of these services has been given in Units 20 and 21 but here I hope to suggest to you the place which these services, and the refinements of them made in the 1930s, found in everyday living accommodation.

Third came the development of new structural techniques. Those made available throughout the 1930s were, in effect, a false dawn for their propagandizers, who, loudly proclaiming the revolution which, say, the Mopin system of construction would bring to building, were unaware that the real changes were made not by concrete but by the services.

Change in attitude

Throughout the 1930s articles regularly appeared on such as the 'Home Page' of the *Evening Standard* either extolling the virtues of continental design or making Wellsian prophecies about the mechanized future to come. An example of this first type was the writer whose subject was 'Family Life in Berlin' where he described with awe the functional severity of the small German flat:

Two bedrooms and a living room show none of the decorative fancy of the English surburban home. Utility is the watchword and aspidistras are banned.
(*Evening Standard*, 26 July 1930, p. 18)

Articles like this appeared with such frequency and were so often filled with equivocal comments such as these that it is clear that the canon of International Style design was at least popularly known in England during the early 1930s even if it was not necessarily admired.

C. Ernest Elcock was a writer of the second type of article in a prophetic vein in the tradition of H. G. Wells or Jules Verne. He was aware that the generalized English historicist architecture was redundant and historically irrelevant. In writing about the look of these flats he anticipated Wells Coates's Isokon Flats (1934) [**Plate 55**] and Connell, Ward and Lucas's Kent House (1935) [**Plate 89**]. Elcock wrote:

The external appearance of the modern flats will not follow any recognized style, and instead of bowdlerised versions of 'Georgian' fronts and 'Mary Ann' backs, will be seen buildings with a life and vigour of their own.
(*Evening Standard*, 7 July 1930, p. 10)

Interestingly, in the period before this was an easy guess Elcock predicted the wide availability of domestic electrical gadgets, but what is most particularly interesting to us is not so much that he predicted the appearance of flats as that he predicted that the homes of the future would be flats. These flats he envisaged would be completely serviced, controlled environments. None of the examples which we are going to look at in this unit reached the stage of refinement which Elcock advocates yet most of them were built at some time after he wrote. Elcock saw the centralized heating and dispersal of hot water as inevitable and that

The preparation of food will be recognised as a chemical process. The kitchen will become a compact and scientifically fitted laboratory.
(*Evening Standard*, 7 July 1930, p. 10)

This, of course, is more the immediate province of Unit 20 but Elcock went on to add that the kitchens of the future would all be fitted with electric cookers, mechnical devices for cutting and mixing food, dishwashers, flush-doored cupboards (these appeared in the Isokon Flats, see **Plate 58**), refrigerators, glazed walls, glazed ceilings and valve-like windows designed not to admit fresh air but to exclude flies and dust. A sort of Corbusian *respiration exacte* would be internally contrived.

You should imagaine that it was with fantastic interiors like this, at least, in mind that the flats which are the subjects of this unit were created.

Meanwhile, at the other end of this decade before the Second World War put a stop to all architectural idealism, and any other sort too, Howard Robertson wrote that,

Nobody today questions the absolute necessity of providing good service quarters, efficiently and comfortably organised both as regards working and amenity. Equally recognised as indispensable are plentiful and well equipped bathrooms and lavatories . . .

rooms well lit and warmed with central heating and the independent auxiliary of gas or electric fires or radiators; systems of construction and methods of finishing minimising noise and vibration from neighbours, the exterior, and the impact of mechanical services such as pipes, lifts, and all working plant including the stoking mechanism of boilers where gas, oil, or electricity are not employed as fuel. Granted these essentials, and adding to them a certain quota of luxury equipment, such as radio and television wiring and service, plant for water softening, central letter and dust chutes, intercommunicating phones, controlled ventilation and air-conditioning, we have a list of desiderata increasingly placed at the disposition of tenants.

(Howard Robertson, *Flats*, Ascot Gas Water Company Ltd., London, 1938)

We can take Robertson's point of view as typical—if idealistic—of the time. Obviously, few people's resources would extend to such fanciful limits as his but the quotation is useful in that it shows what was, at least theoretically, available to flat dwellers in the later 1930s.

To comprehend the abyss between what was possible and what was likely there is the work of an altogether more practical commentator on flats, H. Ingham Ashworth. Ashworth as we have seen was no flat romantic and his vision and pronouncements on the subject, while not as exciting as Robertson's, have the dull ring of truth to them.

Despite Robertson's dream Ashworth could write only two years before that 'the initial capital cost of mechanical equipment is relatively small in relation to the capital cost of the building'[1] when considering a general proposal concerning the design of a block of flats. Because of this, Ashworth thought, the architect's choice of mechanical equipment should be made with exquisite care. Lifts, sewers and other machinery might pierce the walls or basement slab thereby adding to cost and, because to Ashworth's mentality automation was still a dare, he warned of complacency caused by the 'automatic' label and encourage architects to think twice before installing expensive equipment which was liable, in any case, to go wrong and make still greater demands on finance by requiring constant servicing.

Services: Central heating and hot water

The placing of the boilers and the disposition of the pipes and radiators can positively effect the design of the building. Bear in mind when you read the following quotation the considerations which an architect working in the 1930s had to make when designing his building. In the first age of automated equipment such advice would have been far from commonplace:

[The Heating Chamber] . . . should be of ample size and preferably of good shape, i.e. not full of awkward angles and recesses, &c., which would necessitate a complicated layout. A square or rectangular shape would appear to be the most satisfactory.

The possible available positions for the flue will be one of the deciding factors. The heating chamber should be easy of access both for the adequate supervision and the supply of fuel.

As much height as possible should be obtained to allow the metal ducts, pipe-runs, etc. . . .

Suitable means of access for the fitting of new boilers or accessories must be considered.

Alternative means of escape should be provided.

(Ashworth, H. I., *op. cit.*, pp. 64–5)

So you can see that the design of a mere boiler room was no simple thing. Not only this, but there had to be space too for fuel storage and if the fuel specified was solid, provision had to be made for keeping it dry. In this respect, at least, oil was superior to coal and as well as that its supply was easier to automate causing greater latitude of planning to be employed and minimizing dirt. Automatic feeds for solid fuel (consisting of a hopper emptied by a rotating screw) existed but they were both expensive and unreliable.

Electricity for lighting and water heating

Electricity, of course, as a source of both power and heat had infinite advantages over its rivals in that it was clean, easy to regulate and, best of all, required no storage space. It was, however very expensive, and even in 1936 fuel costs were a source of persistent financial discomfort.

Electricity's advantages were seen only by those with a futuristic vision, for in the 1930s the position of electricity in the world was by no means firmly established and it still had about it something of the atmosphere of gimcrackery. Planning for electricity was not easy for there was no national grid and electricity was supplied—with varying degrees of reliability—by different companies. The type of electricity was not even standardized: two- and three-wire DC and single, two- and three-phase AC all existed side-by-side for lighting and were supplied at 230V while for serious power applications 400V AC current was used.

Although electric plant is almost 100% efficient it was because of these drawbacks that electricity had few friends in the 1930s.

It had, of course, won almost complete acceptance as a source of lighting (the average house requiring 1,500–2,000 hours of artificial light a year made the obvious hygienic and atmospheric advantages of electricity over gas very attractive) but had yet to establish its place in the everyday home. Lack of standardized supply and expense were its main enemies; electricity generally cost $\frac{1}{2}$–$\frac{3}{4}$d per unit in the mid 1930s but electric heating was only a really practicable proposition if the unit cost dropped to $\frac{3}{4}$d at 1937 values. A letter published in late 1937 by *The Times* as part of the correspondence between Sir Denis Maine-

[1] H. Ingham Ashworth, *Flats—Design and Equipment*, Pitman, 1936, p. 64.

Wilson, Governor of The Gas Light and Coke Co. Ltd., and the journalist Ian Hamilton, the author of a so-called 'scurrilous' article 'The All-Electric Flat' written to draw attention to the service benefits which electricity could provide, illustrates this point precisely. Naturally, following Hamilton's article, Sir Denis Maine-Wilson quickly (and repeatedly) rose to the defence of the interests of his industry. His last letter of the correspondence gives us a clear idea of the disadvantages which electricity was considered to have had in the 1930s:

> If we are to believe Mr Hamilton, a flat so equipped is all-electric simply because any tenant with a superfluity of time and money could ignore the main fuel appliance provided for her (the combination coal-grate-water heater) and spend her shillings on continuous 'all electric' heating, or her time in ladling electrically heated water from her wash copper into her bath, . . . and (presumably) carrying it in saucepans-full to the sink where Mr Hamilton has provided her with no hot water. . . . Those landlords who are in the best position to know where this particular shoe pinches (the boroughs owning their own electrical undertakings) are the most careful to install, in their 'all electric' dwellings, a protection for their consumers and themselves in the shape of a good, solid, black coal range.
>
> (*The Times*, Wednesday, 27 October 1937, p. 10d)

Because of the chaotic organization of the electricity generating companies they were often unable to meet the demand and power-cuts were frequent; as late as 1937 there was no smoothly organized manner of electricity supply and relatively few housing authorities anticipated its use. In 1930 gas light was still cheaper (and more popular!) than electricity because with its new automatic switches it rivalled the convenience of electricity and gas lights no longer required a pilot. Only progressive local authorities such as those at Liverpool and London made early experiments with electric lighting.

Heat distribution

Of the two types of device available in the 1930s for distributing heat from high-temperature water, the radiator was the usual one to find in medium-rental flats while the more efficient and costly panel system was generally restricted only to high-rental properties. Strictly speaking, of course, these 'radiators' are not radiators at all because they distribute 85% of their heat by convection with only the remaining 15% distributed directly by radiation. (Radiation is the direct heating of the air by radiant heat from a hot object; convection is the movement of hot air from one part of a room to another.) Because of this, radiators were usually placed underneath windows where the rise of the convected currents of air would help to eliminate down-draughts from the windows. Paint always diminishes the performance of radiators by up to 15%; if appearance demands that they should be painted, metallic paints like aluminium and bronze should be avoided because their effect is to cut down heat discharge by up to 30%. The amount of radiator area needed was usually calculated on the basis of 14 $ft.^2$ of radiator for every 1,000 $ft.^3$ of space on the ground floor, and 25 $ft.^2$ of radiator for every 1,000 $ft.^3$ on the upper floors.

Low-pressure hot-water installation

In a low-pressure system the water is circulated by gravity; sometimes aided by pumps. Because of the high cost of power supply to electric pumps their inclusion in a system could only be justified if, without them, even more expensive wide bore pipes were needed. Low-pressure systems required the siting of the water tank on the roof.

Lifts

Throughout the nineteenth century English conservatism was unwilling to accept the lift. In 1884 the cost of a lift for a six-storey block was about £4,000–5,000 for installation plus an annual charge of about £800 to cover the costs of maintenance and the water rate for the hydraulic system and the attendant's wages. Although Yorke and Gibberd argued that in a building more than three storeys tall lifts were necessary, the conservative developer traditionally argued that five-storey buildings could be built without lifts at no detriment to the possibility of getting residents, but generally the top floors of tall buildings without lifts had to be let at lower rates than the ground floors in order to induce the less energetic residents to take up occupation there.

In the 1930s lifts still had high capital and maintenance costs but were beginning to find more favour with landlords who were aware that they could soon write off the expense of the lift against the higher rents they would be able to charge for the upper floors. Regulations required that the number of lifts for a given block of flats be calculated on the basis of evacuating all the occupants above first-floor level in one hour and, in less hectic times, on the practical desirability of not having to wait for a lift for more than 35 seconds.

The time for a round trip by lift could be calculated with the equation

$$T = H(120/R + 0.57) \text{ seconds} \quad T = \text{time}$$
$$H = \text{vertical run}$$
$$R = \text{speed in ft. min}^{-1}$$

The speeds of lifts in five-storey buildings were, therefore, from 100–200 ft. min^{-1} and in six- to ten-storey buildings from 200–350 ft. min^{-1}. The American express lifts were unknown in England before the repeal of the *London Building Act* which had limited the very height of the buildings merely to the required initial clear run for an express lift service.

The planning difficulties which lifts involved were, besides penetration of the basement slab, the bulge or penthouse on the roof to house the winding gear. Although the gear could theoretically be stored in the basement this could interfere with boiler space and the roof installation required 30% less cable and caused the equipment less wear-and-tear. If, however, the building was a steel-framed one, having the winding gear on the roof could lead to a transmission of vibration throughout the whole building. All these factors had to be borne in mind by an architect before he was able to decide on the installation of lifts in his building.

Refuse

The increasing number of flats meant, in turn, that increasing research was necessary into the problem of waste disposal. The two most primitive waste-disposal systems available in the 1930s were: (*a*) the dustbin and (*b*) the chute. To provide a really satisfactory service, dustbins require separate lifts of their own so their apparent economy is merely illusory. The Bickenhall Mansion Flats off Baker Street had exposed service lifts running up the inside of the court staffed by porters whose job it was to empty the residents' bins. Besides this, bins are laborious to manoeuvre and unhygienic as waste vehicles.

Figure 14 The Shelvoke and Drewry container system

Chutes are the more preferable alternative and in medium- high-rental flats became more and more common throughout the course of the century. One chute could serve up to twenty flats and, although expensive in initial construction, has an almost indefinite life.

In designing a waste chute the architect has to take into account that no smells must escape from the bottom end and that the chute should be made of material that is both durable and easy to clean: glazed stoneware is ideal but expensive while galvanized iron is cheap and efficient but transmits noise.

An innovation in the collecting of refuse from blocks of flats was made by the English firm, Shelvoke and Drewery Ltd. of Letchworth [**Fig. 14**].

This firm still makes the majority of local authority dustbin lorries and their 1936 system had much in common with the normal dustbin system although its scale was larger. The system used containers which were collected daily by lorries which left behind an empty container to be filled over the following day. This system, which had, clearly, to be used in conjunction with a chute, was neat and efficient but expensive because the lorries had to make numbers of single journeys.

The most civilized and noteworthy waste-disposal system developed in the 1930s was that of *Etablissements Garchey* of Paris. Following its influential appearance in Beaudoin and Lods's idealistic Cité de la Muette it was widely adopted for use in working-class flats in France and even found its way to England [**Figs. 15–16**].

Figure 15 Sectional drawing of the Garchey *system of waste disposal*

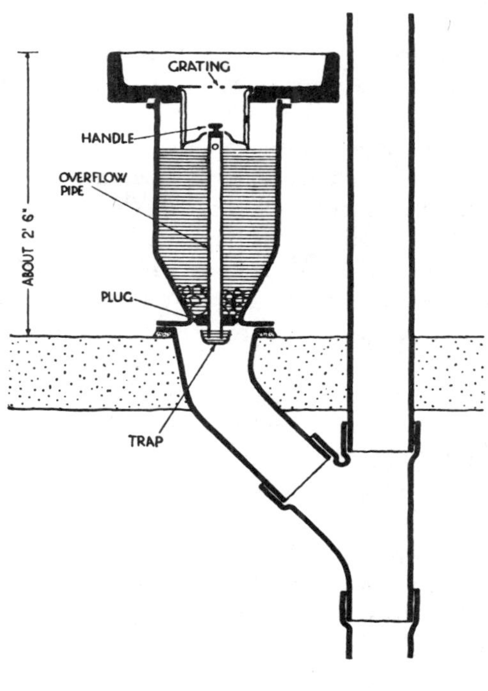

Commenting on the Garchey system the *Journal of the RIBA* said that 'usually the dustbin is tolerated as a necessary evil, but it remains an evil'.[1] (This makes an important point in that all the service innovations which have affected buildings in this century are, in effect, simple principles made efficient by the application of engineering principles. From the dustbin developed the water-carriage system of waste disposal and the Garchey system made another advance over this.)

The Garchey system combined the water-carriage technique with a vacuum which drew the accumulated refuse to destruction. The Garchey system requires a large, clumsy sanitary fitting to be placed under each sink unit. Each sink has a movable grating which can be lifted to deposit all kitchen refuse (except, of course, large solid objects like tin cans and cardboard boxes). The rubbish settles in the sanitary fitting which is filled with water, and when sufficient has accumulated the handle below the grating is raised and the vacuum created flushes the whole mess into the down pipe. The force of the vacuum ensures that a degree of cleanliness is maintained and the different seals on the unit ensure that no smells penetrate the kitchen. The soilstacks feed into the basement sumps where the accumulated refuse is taken to a disposal station. The liquid which is in the sanitary fitting is drawn off to a separate sewer. The solid waste is centrifugally dried ('hydroextracture' was the futuristic term used by Garchey's exponents) and then burnt in a basement furnace whose excess heat is used to drive the building's plant. At the Chatenay Malabry scheme near Paris the heat derived from the Garchey disposal system was used to heat the swimming pool.

The Garchey system's two major advantages were that the refuse was never exposed to the air and immediately out of sight, and that it was economical in the use of labour. Naturally, its disadvantage was that its capital cost was high and while its mechanics were simple by our standards they were, in the 1930s, suspiciously complicated.

At Drancy the rubbish which the Garchey system could not tackle was disposed of through chutes requiring an extra capital investment. In England, before the Garchey system was used in R. A. H. Livett's revolutionary Quarry Hill Estate at Leeds, 1934–41, the usual system had been that used at, for instance, the Hornsey Rise and Shore Estate, Hackney, 1928, where the refuse from the various floors was disposed of through letter-box like orifices to travel down 12 in. glazed soilstacks. These pipes were cased in 4½ in. brickwork and, to prevent odour, were ventilated by pipes going up to the roof.

Even in advanced housing projects in this country like Kensal House, rubbish had to be carried out in dustbins. This, however, was not altogether unusual, for even the most apparently progressive housing schemes were in their essential nature conservative. Problems of separating both kitchen and human waste from living areas have often beset flat designers. Ventilation flues had to be built for bathroom and WC wherever it was not possible to place these 'human service' areas on the exterior to achieve natural ventilation. You should remember that it is decisions which are as mundane as this which materially affect the shape of flats.

Structural innovations

Not only in England, but throughout Europe, the building trade has been notably resistant to innovation. The strength of the building trade unions inhibited the introduction of many structural innovations. Furthermore, as Sigfried Giedion pointed out in reference to the generalized conservatism of the building industry:

> Architecture is almost the last of the big productive trades to change over from handicraft to industrial production. At present, there are no more than the very first steps in this direction. The reasons for which since the beginning of the industrial era building has not kept abreast of the evolution of other branches (traffic and the textile machinery industries, for instance) are of various kinds. Economical reasons and considerations of organisation were not the least factors in the lagging behind, but the foremost ones are certain prejudices, which are again and again aired when people are out to thwart architectural development.
>
> (Sigfried Giedion, *'Die Internationalen Kongresse fur Neues Bauen'*, CIAM Zurich/Hoffman (Stuttgart), p. vii)

Figure 16 Installation of the Garchey *system*

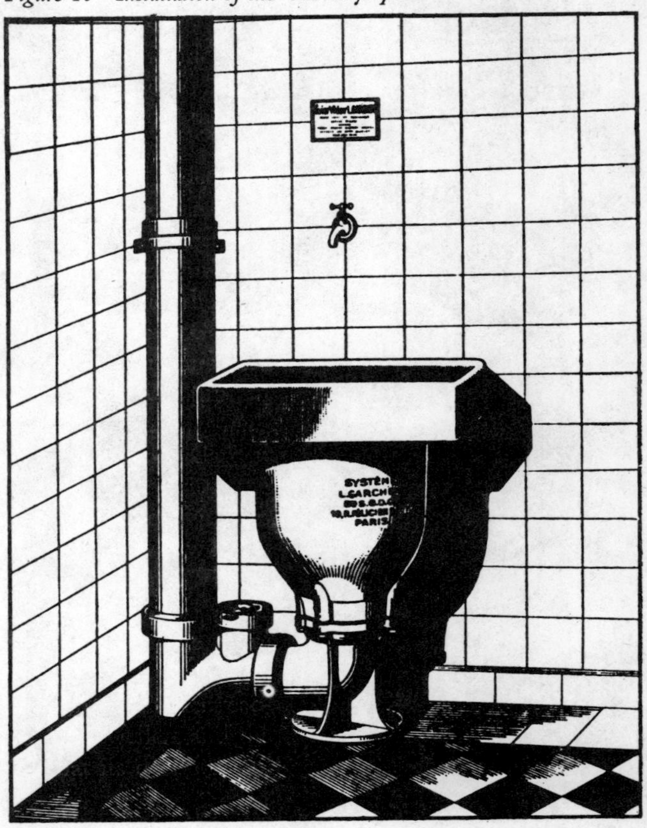

[1] *Journal of the RIBA*, 14 April, 1934, p. 576.

And Wells Coates, too, had something to say on the industrialization of building techniques:

Building costs too much. Why? Because it has never been properly related to the forms, processes and economies of large-scale power production.
(Wells Coates, *Architectural Association Journal* LIII, April 1938, p. 614)

It is a noteworthy paradox that in the 1930s industrialization, before it met its Waterloo in the fashionable disenchantment of the opinion-mongers, could be thought of by a radical like Coates as the saving hope for humanity. Coates was an engineer and the elegant success of mass production was a principle which he never tired of propagandizing. He even had a vision of dwellings dropping off the ends of production lines but, he hoped, they would be modern flats not reactionary semi-detached houses!

So, both Sigfried Giedion and Wells Coates, among others, hoped to see a revolution in building techniques so that architecture could more readily serve humanity. Similarly, in his book *Anticipations*, published in 1902, H. G. Wells had written:

I find it incredible that there will not be a sweeping revolution in the methods of building during the next century. A few energetic men might at any time set out to alter this.
(Cited in Richard Moore, 'An Early System of Large Panel Building, in *Journal of the RIBA*, Sept. 1969, pp. 383–6)

This has been both right and wrong, for the century has seen many structural innovations, some of which will be the subjects of this section, but because building is a traditionally labour-intensive industry it has always resisted what changes in technique might put employment at risk. Even today domestic building is hardly affected by industrialization and this was even more the case in the 1920s and 1930s: it is almost comic to look at contemporary photographs of a Le Corbusier villa proceeding to its machine-like shape inch-by-inch as artisans and craftsmen lovingly apply the machine-finish rendering while, within, other craftsmen are carefully tiling the kitchen and bathroom!

Prefabrication

The major innovations in structural engineering in this century have come from the continent but an intriguing early experiment, the direct antecedent of an influential French system, can claim England as its home. Remember that, at this time, the conventional type of construction would have been simple brick facing and load-bearing walls with wooden floors.

This was Brodie's large-panel system. In Liverpool, in 1904, the City Engineer, J. A. Brodie, erected a block of tenement flats on the Eldon Street site near the city centre. They were of an advanced plan including for each of twelve flats a living room, two bedrooms, scullery, WC and refuse chute. There was a communal playground on the roof before Le Corbusier had thought of it but the most important single feature of interest was the unique method of construction. Brodie described his own system as follows:

The principle adopted for the construction of each room in the building has been that of a dove-tailed box—each of the four sides, the floor and ceiling of a room consisting of one concrete slab made in a mould at a depot . . . whence, after maturing, it was conveyed behind a traction engine to the site and erected in position.
Report of the City Engineer, 22 April 1905, cited in Moore, *op. cit.*

The interesting system differed in that the large panels were not made on the site but at a distant factory and had to be transported to the scene of the building. Before building the Eldon Street flats Brodie had experimented with his system at a Cottage in Everton; an exhibit at the Cheap Cottage Exhibition in Letchworth and at the Liverpool Corporation Stables in Walton.

Brodie's vision was breathtakingly advanced for the flats were to be a totally designed whole. All the concrete panels were reinforced by flat metal mesh; the floors had an inlaid timber finish (presumably from the shuttering); some panels even had integrated colouring. Where panels were damaged either in manufacture or in transport, they were replaced by rolled-steel joists supporting smaller slabs. In the scullery there was an L-shaped pre-cast panel which held a pre-cast concrete sink. There were other designed-in recesses to accommodate the services. The windows and the internal doors fitted directly into the slabs with the hinges cast directly into the concrete.

John Alexander Brodie (1858–1934) was an interesting man in his own right. Among his achievements he could count being the Bilbao Harbour Master at the age of just twenty-four and the inventing of football goal nets at the age of thirty-one. He also was responsible for the planning of the famous East Lancashire Road. He became the Liverpool City Engineer at the age of forty and he patented his 'Liverpool System' of large panel construction in March 1901.

Brodie's system depended, of course, on the use of ferro-concrete. Interestingly, this material had been introduced to this country by L. G. Mouchel's work in Liverpool and Brodie had himself used Hennebique's system in some of his early work for the corporation. It seems likely that Brodie developed his ideas on concrete prefabrication from his work at the Bilbao docks where he had used gantry cranes to assemble dock buildings. It was the obvious extension of this practice to apply it to domestic building. The planning, economic and time advantages are clear. Brodie said that:

By this mode of procedure, and in consequence of the rapid erection possible, according to my invention, I meet the great difficulty at present experienced in dealing with the masses rendered homeless when large areas are dealt with *en bloc*.

(Moore, *op. cit.*, p. 385)

and because he was not afraid to let his experiments be known publicly he enjoyed an extensive popular reputation for his innovations. His invention was reported to the city's housing committee in February 1903, and it was said that other local authorities were anxiously awaiting the results of his experiments. The Local Government Board (the creators of the Tudor Walters Report) soon approved of his scheme and production of his concrete slabs began at his experimental site at Lobbs Quarry, Everton.

There were initial troubles with the workmen who had reservations about the new system: they felt unsure and unsafe working without the traditional scaffolding and harboured primitive fears about the rightness of slotting together a building. To satisfy these reservations a bye-law was introduced which required the design thickness of the walls to be doubled. However, despite these setbacks, all the slabs at the Eldon Street site were in position by November 1904, but the cost for the project had more than tripled from £1,230 to £4,072.

However, news of Brodie's invention and its successful application reached as far as the USA where an eighteen-storey block built on the 'Liverpool System' was projected and between 1906 and 1921 an American architect called Grosvenor Atterbury developed Brodie's invention by using battery casting and steam curing of the concrete panels. By a strange historical accident it was by this route that the system found its way back to Europe where, for instance, the Cambridge Corporation adopted the similar Dutch system of large panel building.

The relevance of this long account of an obscure experiment in building technique in Liverpool at the turn of the century is to demonstrate that Brodie's early system had many similarities with the much better known French Mopin system. The French engineer was not working alone: his invention was part of an already established tradition of large-panel building.

The Mopin system

The Mopin system saw the first realization of Henry Ford's mass production techniques in building. The essential difference between the systems of Brodie and Mopin was that in the one case the large panels were fabricated at a distant site and transported to the building area while, in the other, the panels were fabricated at the actual site of the building.

The advantages of the Mopin system of large-panel building were that the system was non-specific and employed basic units of construction which could be applied to virtually any project; its elasticity of use allowed it to be used by existing organized labour; it was cheaper than brick (but had similar fire-resistance) and it did not require the same amount of scaffolding or site preparation as a conventional building scheme.

Its first popular application was at the pilot scheme for the Cité de la Muette, the Cité du Champs des Oiseaux near Paris. Both these schemes were designed by Beaudoin and Lods and differed from Brodie's modest twelve-flat project in their magnificence: the earlier scheme was budgeted at £400,000, the later one at £1,200,000.

The system employed small pre-cast reinforced concrete units for attachment to a steel framework.

The system's singular advantage was in weight saving: neither the concrete nor the steel units weighed more than 200–250 lb. Besides having barely any need for scaffolding, the Mopin system did away with the need of shuttering (the panels were pre-cast before assembly), heavy hoists and much site equipment, because the factory-made components of the building were all highly finished.

The strength of the structure was dependent on the iron and the steel, a principle which the building regulations of Britain viewed with the gravest suspicion. Safety regulations in Europe have always been more lax than in England but provision was nevertheless made for the structural steelwork to be protected by wet-poured concrete, particularly at its bolted joints.

Fig. 17 a–f shows how the prefabricated units act as moulds for the concrete, which was both protective and structural. The outer wall was made of T-section reinforced concrete beams set vertically. There were rods projecting from these units at both the top and the bottom and they were bent round the steel members and finally fixed by the poured concrete on setting.

The actual large panels of the Mopin system were made of *vibrated concrete* cast in metal moulds fixed on a moving table. Thus the vibration of the setting concrete ensures a good dense mixture and a total filling of voids. This enabled a relatively dry mix to be used and is, incidentally, the usual way of making paving slabs in England.

In the Beaudoin and Lods scheme at Drancy the Mopin slabs were finished with a rough aggregate of Carrara marble. This was done purely for aesthetic effect and while it did not meet with enthusiasm from English commentators, it did at least demonstrate the visual possibilities of the system.

The average weight of a Mopin system wall was 41 lb. ft.$^{-2}$ and the thermal conductivity of the walling was the equivalent of 18 in. of brickwork.

In 1934, when the first article on the Mopin system appeared in a British journal,[1] it could not yet be considered for English applications because it contravened the existing legislation. However, the system did have its

[1] 'The Mopin System of Construction', *Journal of RIBA*, 24 March 1934, pp. 518–21.

Figure 17 The Mopin System

(a) Typical horizontal section through wall showing (A) T-sectioned outer wall members, (B) inner wall of circular concrete, (C) typical light stanchion, (D) concrete filling.

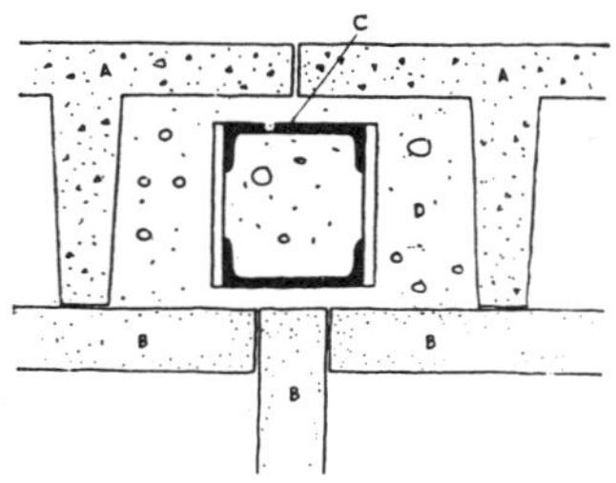

(b) Diagrammatic horizontal section of steelwork showing (A) stanchion, (B) main wall beam, (C) two floor beams cleated to (B).

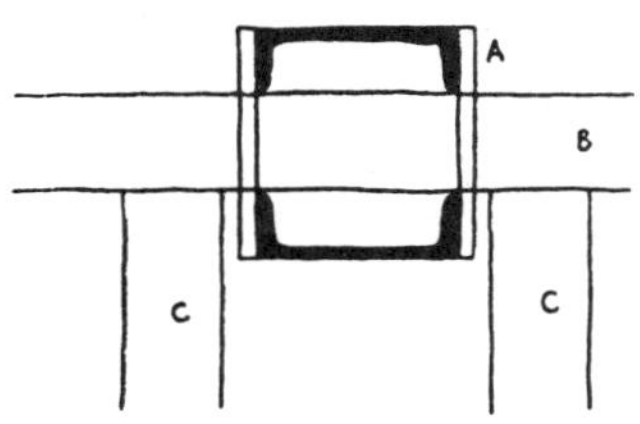

(c) Sketch of typical vibrated concrete outer wall unit showing (A) holes for stirrups.

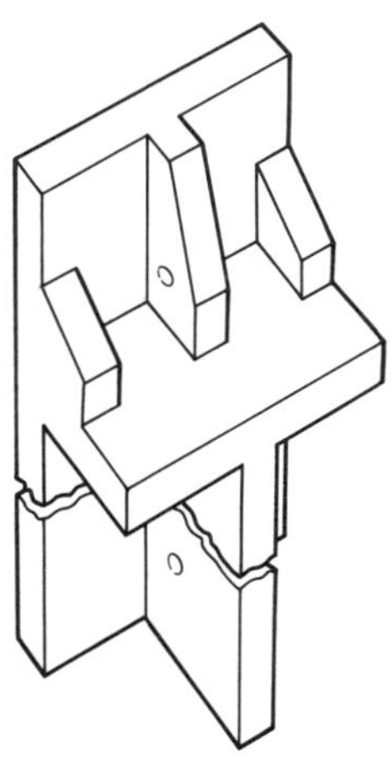

(d) Assembling the walls. Vertical section showing (A) lower wall unhooked to horizontal joist and (B) a pre-cast floor slab and (C) a wood joist for the sub-ceiling which holds (D) a slotted concrete distance piece.

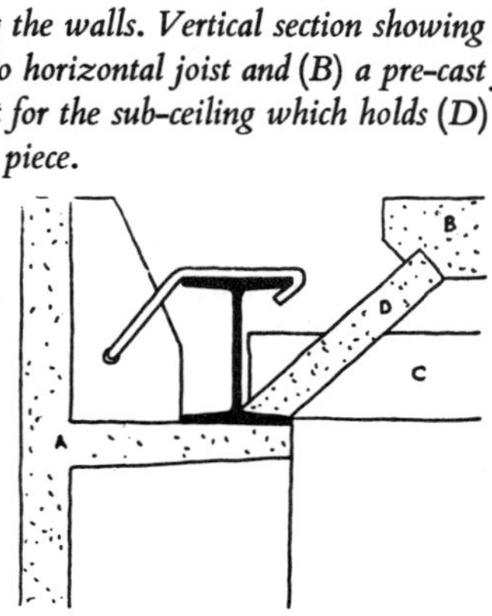

(e) Vertical section showing an upper wall unit (A) with hooks (B) hung over a continuous rod.

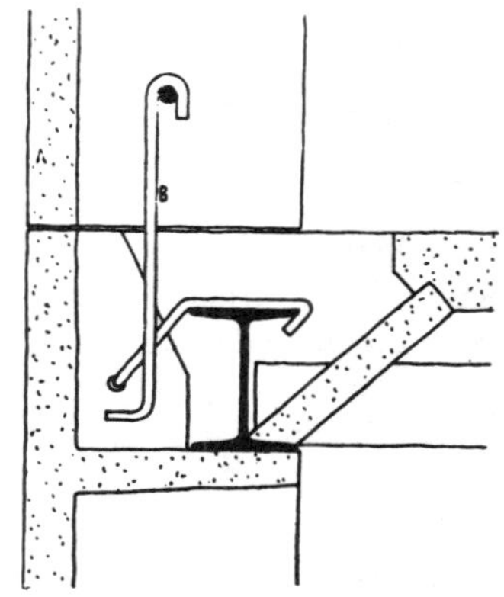

(f) Vertical section showing the concrete filling (A). A single board (B) acts as temporary shuttering.

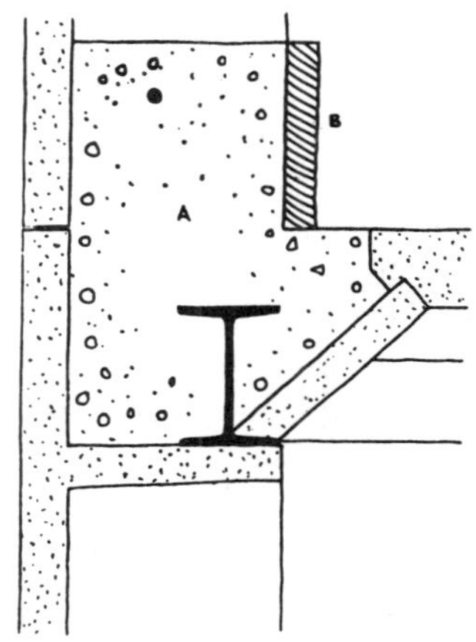

advantages: (i) the necessarily repetitive units enforced a conceptual and aesthetic unity, (ii) no haphazard techniques were possible and the whole building project had to be planned elaborately from the outset, (iii) the organization of work could be rationalized, (iv) there was no plaster or mortar to dry out and (v) the prefabrication site could be turned into a tennis court or other recreational area after the departure of the builders. Combined with its elegant practicality, these factors attracted Livett and the Leeds City Architects' Department to adopt the Mopin system for their Quarry Hill flat housing scheme. It is entirely appropriate that what was at the time the most advanced and ambitious development of flats in England should employ the most advanced continental techniques.

Fig. 17e shows how the pre-cast wall units are attached to the framework in the Mopin system and how the units act as moulds into which is poured the concrete to case the steel.

When the steel frame of the building has been erected the floor units are then put into place and the wooden sub-ceiling joints are hung on the lower flanges of the rolled-steel joists.

Fig. 17d shows the top of an outer wall section hooked on to a rolled-steel joist; **Fig. 17f** shows a board in place to act as a temporary means of shuttering for the fresh concrete which encases the steelwork.

Although the Mopin system was the most influential large-panel building system to appear in the 1930s it was not the only one.

The Times of 15 May 1936 reported an innovation in unitary construction being tried out at Apsley House, Finchley Road, where concrete units which were made on the site were used in the building. However, the concrete here was disguised as bricks. Each slab measured 4 ft. × 5 ft. × 2 in. and after they had been placed in position the necessary timber shuttering was placed behind them and the concrete which was to form the bulk of the wall was poured into place. When this concrete dried the shuttering was removed, leaving a solid wall which required no structural steel-work.

This method had similar advantages to the Mopin system in reducing building costs and accelerating the speed of building. Like the Mopin system, it also offered the benefits of light construction, high fire resistance and protection from aircraft and traffic noise. However, it is interesting to note that the application of unitary construction to a non-working class building had, perforce, to avoid the risqué appearance of naked concrete which, in 1936, was already beginning to have social associations and it was considered necessary to hide the nature of the material behind a disguise of brickwork.

These associations which naked concrete was developing for itself were largely the product of the influence of the continental visionary theorists and the socialist housing associations among the arbiters of taste in England.

2 The political example

G. Grey Wornum, the architect of the RIBA building in Portland Place and a doyen of the traditional English architectural establishment, had been present at the CIAM's conference at Frankfurt. Now Wornum, while a traditionalist, was not actively antagonistic to foreign architecture and we can take his slightly amused attitude to Le Corbusier as typical of the reaction of non-progressive architects to the infiltration of modernist ideas into housing. Wornum reported that:

> Le Corbusier was advocating for tenements that all windows should be hermetically sealed and that . . . 'l'air exacte' should be pumped into rooms so as to give the benefit of the purest air science could desire. He further advocated as a solution of the road traffic problem that roads should be made in place of approach balconies at every floor level.
>
> (G. Grey Wornum 'Modern Flats', *Journal of the RIBA*, 1931, p. 441)

You can imagine the wonder with which Wornum regarded these outlandish proposals; he certainly was not unsympathetic to them for he was a man of learning and taste who was willing to attest to the example of Berlin's and Vienna's housing schemes (although he thought that German architecture 'lacked charm') and he showed that he was familiar with continental developments by using illustrations from *Wasmuths Monatshefte* in his articles. However, he plainly did not take Le Corbusier seriously and in his opinion that the French and the Germans would have benefited from experience of the quality of English flats he was perhaps right.

Wornum had himself travelled to Vienna and he was plainly unimpressed by the paragons of Austrian housing. We have already mentioned the absence of lifts in the Viennese flats, and their generally inferior standard of finish and equipment was in marked contrast to their apparent grandeur. Wornum correctly stated that the typical Viennese worker's flat would just not be acceptable in England. Certainly, the Viennese were themselves aware of their failings. It was thought, for instance, in 1932 that

> It is manifestly better to give to tens of thousands of down-trodden human beings a small, sunny and modest home . . . than to provide a considerably smaller number of families with roomy flats having their own private bathroom, central heating, hot water supply and so on.
>
> (*Wohnen und Bauen* (International Housing Assoc.), vol. IV, No. 5/6, 1932, p. 201)

This attitude on the behalf of the Viennese authorities explains why they were able to provide such massive rehousing for a relatively modest cost. The Germans, too, skimped on fittings in their flats and many German Siedlungen had no provision for central heating or hot water, though many, such as Bruno Taut's Britz Siedlung, had advanced communal laundry facilities. So you can see that on the one hand the attitude to continental architecture in the 1930s was certainly not one of unreserved admiration. Even the quiet Dutch did not escape criticism for the preponderance of speculators over architects in that country where architects were paid by the yard of façade dreamed up and where, like Austria and Germany, the flats often had poor accommodation and finish they were objects of criticism to English commentators.

Howard Robertson, in the Ascot book of flats, supported this point of view when he wrote that

> It may be accepted, however, that the general standard of housing, as far as accommodation is concerned, is still higher in England than in most European countries.
>
> ('The Design of Continental Flats', *Ascot*, 1938, p. 43)

The underlying implication of this was, of course, that British flatted housing was aesthetically inferior to its continental rivals. Even in flats the English have an urge to recreate vernacular styles and the contest between cottage and flat, while not perfectly resolved, was sometime almost compromised in the same building! A similar competition was in hand in Europe too, particularly in the Nordic countries: the Copenhagen municipal authorities had experimented with cottages but, finding them too costly, reverted to the four- or five-storey block as the standard housing unit for the working classes while, conversely, under Hitler the 'Jewish' International Style was at first 'Aryanized' by the addition of pitched roofs and finally replaced by a reversal of housing policy and the readoption of the cottage. The Nazis found the associations of the flatted superblock too ideologically impure and too charged with the force of *Kunstbolschewismus* to be tolerated in their form of planned economy. The actual responsibility for the branding of the superblock with the associations of progressive politics and internationalism must lie with the Austrians.

The Viennese provided Europe with the most notable exemplar of empirical social and housing planning. The city's socialist administration carried out its Faustian scheme, while all the time keeping an eye on petty economies like bathrooms and heating, with an almost total disregard for the established rules of economics. From 1920 onwards (when the programme began) they ignored the accountant's golden rule of achieving a balance between investment and return.

This brave new approach was forced upon the city's administration by the results of the First World War. Austria, newly created, was trapped within Treaty of Versailles frontiers and a population way beyond her sources available to provide for it. The knife-edged balance could only be maintained by the export of industrial products. Trapped in a vicious circle of keeping wages low to keep the price of goods down the Austrians found that the workers were unable to pay high rents thereby necessitating the creation of massive state-subsidized (if that is the right expression for financing *à fonds perdu*) housing, and by special graduated taxes which placed the burden of payment on the wealthy classes. For instance, in Vienna the residents of the 527,730 cheap dwellings paid just 23% of the total housing rate while the 3,470 more wealthy residents (in terms of individual dwellings) paid 44% of the rate.

The monumental building scheme, once financed, was helped in the formation of its character by the repeal of the old *Wiener Bauordnung* (Vienna Building Regulation) which had permitted up to 85% of an available site to be built upon. It was partially as a reaction to the implied overcrowding that this regulation encouraged that the new Viennese superblocks achieved a distinctively airy layout: the Washington-Hof flats for instance only covered 28% of their site.

The new regulations replacing the old *Bauordnung* laid down that the angle of incidence for light should be at least 45° thus achieving the much-vaunted 'sunny aspect', and that the old Viennese planning custom of grouping all WCs on the one floor of a tenement shared by up to twenty kitchen doors be replaced, as a matter of revolutionary importance, by an individual WC to each flat.

The actual Viennese achievement was that the Viennese Municipal authorities produced between 1919 and 1934 an unstable marriage of Wagnerian scale and conception with socialist empirical planning and reorganization. Paradoxically, the defiantly named Karl-Marx-Hof and Liebknechthof flats were, despite the overt inclinations of the socialist administration's *Wohnungspolitik* (Housing Policy), created to solve a really rather prosaic capitalist economic problem.

Under the post-war reorganization Vienna became a state rather than an individual city and the consequent administrative changes enabled the city to conceptualize their new approach to housing policy. Vienna undertook its scheme with the aid of Adolf Loos, Gustav Scheu and Max Ermers. All of these architects were familiar with the traditions and innovations of English housing having each been schooled when the influence of the English Arts and Crafts Movement was at its height and, significantly, each had been working for the Austrian Garden Cities Association. We shall see in Unit 23 that the apparently paradoxical association of garden city and flat—they are different solutions to the same problem—in fact share a lot of common theoretical ground and when projected their lines do not meet at infinity but quite close to earth.

Both movements shared a slightly Messianic idealism and it was this very idealism which made the Viennese Social-Democrats invite the Garden City Association to participate in their scheme.

We have seen elsewhere in this unit that the decision to build flats or to build single-family cottages is not a straightforward but, rather, a vexed one. Generally. in England the cottage dwelling has been favoured in view both of its symbolic 'pastoral' associations and the real economics of servicing which it offers. Where Garden City Associations had influence, the cottage solution to the housing problem was often offered, and it was thus in Vienna where the cottage supporters, the *Siedlungs-und-Kleingarten-Verband*, (Community and Back Garden Group) were locked in ideological struggle with the supporters of the *Zinskaserne* (rent-barracks), the advocates of the flat solution. As we have seen, the day was won by the flat proponents and between 1919 and 1934 Vienna built 68,000 new dwellings: 3,000 were flats and 5,000 were cottage Siedlungen. Almost 300,000 people were rehoused and such was the degree of social conscience exercised by the municipality that constant consumer reaction verdicts were required from the flat dwellers and the municipality was eventually satisfied that its decision had been the correct one.

Figure 18 Karl Ehn, the Karl-Marx-Hof, Vienna, 1927, plan

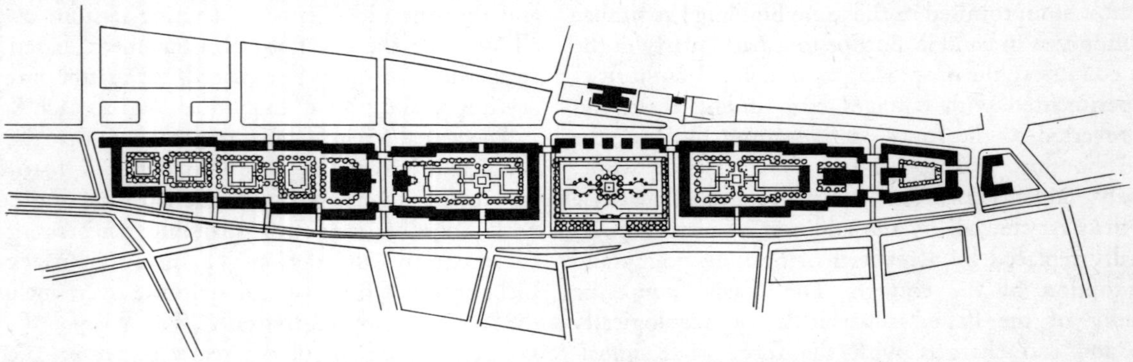

It was between 1923 and 1934 that the wave of superblock building took place, when Vienna built 400 blocks ranging in size from a modest twenty units to an unbelievably massive 1,600—the famous Karl-Marx-Hof designed by Karl Ehn in 1927. The other well-known Viennese superblocks included Fuchsenfeldhof (Schmid and Aichinger) 1922, Reumannshof (Gessner) 1924, George-Washington-Hof, Otto-Haas-Hof (Dirnhuber, Schuster, Loos and Lihotzky) 1924, Winarskyhof (Behrens, Frank, Hoffmann, Strnad and Wlach) 1924, and Paul-Speiser-Hof (Scheffel, Glaser, Lichtblau and Bauer) 1929. Karplus's Ditleshof of 1928 and Dorfmeister's flats in the Döblinger Gürtrel of 1925 are illustrated in **Plates 66** and **67**.

Many of these blocks, though skimped internally by the best English standards, having no lifts and portable shower cabinets in place of baths, did include many communal amenities appropriate to the ideological tinge of the rehousing programme. There were children's playgrounds, paddling pools, meeting halls, libraries, baths, co-operative stores, mechanized laundries, kindergartens and mothercraft centres.

The general style of the buildings was *moderne* rather than modern but, perhaps only on account of the monumentality of the project, won fulsome praise from the many foreign visitors and delegations including one English party who thought that

> To see all this under a summer sky in Vienna is to see a very fine example of humanised architecture.

The first flats contained two rooms and kitchen, and the lucky ones had a balcony. However, under the later economies forced by opposition criticism to the Social-Democrats' public indulgence, the standard of accommodation was reduced to one room and a kitchen living-room. Each separate dwelling cost between 14 and 16 thousand schillings and, through the economies, remarkably low rents were charged which, in fact, averaged about one-fifth of the pre-War rate in the tenement slums.

The outstanding icon of the Viennese programme was the Karl-Marx-Hof of Oberstadtbaurat Ehn. It has a colourful story which is worth recounting.

The Karl-Marx-Hof story

Karl-Marx-Hof was Vienna's largest housing scheme and the only one to achieve an international reputation for the city and its architect, Karl Ehn. The total site area available was 1½ ha of the Hagen meadows stretching for more than one kilometre between the Heiligenstadterstrasse and the embankment of the Franz Josef railway line.

The plan has at its centre a square of 10,500 m² which opens out towards the Heiligenstadterstrasse and, with its gardens, it forms the central formal feature of the plan.

The back of this square, directly in front of the railway station has the highest and grandest buildings of the scheme, the five-storey blocks which form the street which leads to the Hohe Warte (the sports ground) [**Fig. 18**].

Because of the unusual length of the Karl-Marx-Hof it was necessary to include in the plan streets which run at right angles to the axis of the plan. On the plan were included kindergartens, electric laundries, health insurance offices, shops, library and the other communal paraphernalia which went to constitute this mammoth project.

The appearance of the buildings in stylistic terms is as unusual as the size of the colony itself. Ehn certainly achieved an individual and characteristic style, or the Karl-Marx-Hof which owed little to any precedents and gave little to any followers other than, for instance, Lancelot Keay in Liverpool, and R. A. H. Livett in Leeds.

Ehn's style is characterized by massive round arches which pierce the blocks at ground level; by rhythms created by grouped balconies standing proud of the main structure; by tiny formalistic gables piercing the line of the flat roof and by the contrast of texture achieved between brick and rendering (**Plates 68–70**).

Of course, for so large a building any more decorative niceties would be frivolous and the worst that can be said of Ehn's aesthetic creation is that it is unlovely on account of its size alone. His chosen appearance has given to the Karl-Marx-Hof flats the international identity of the cause of socialist housing.

Such a massive scheme can never appear elegant or beautiful and its propagandist nature is emphasized by the raised name in grotesque type inscribed on the central façade. Similarly, the view down the Boschstrasse with its five-storey turreted towers and the range of round-arched entrances was contrived purely for monumental effect rather than beauty. The view at the corner of the Geistinger Gasse is more elegant being lower and having a nice contrast of brick and concrete rendering and a wilful interplay of horizontal rhythms together with decorative features like the three little port-hole windows. However, if Wells Coates's Isokon Flats soon became likened to an ocean liner it is no surprise that the Karl-Marx-Hof's air of impenetrability and enormous presence combined with the political character of its creators lead to it being dubbed the Red Fortress.

The political symbolism of the flat architecture

Vienna's ambitious and statistically successful housing policy came to an end in February 1934 when, following a period of mounting unrest and contrived strikes, a right-wing coup d'état initiated by Dr Dollfuss and enacted by the *Heimwehr* (Homeguard) (who had, by the way, previously taken out insurance policies in the event of civil war, with the Phoenix Insurance Company) led to the fall of Vienna's socialist administration.

Vienna had built twelve times more superblock accommodation than Siedlungen. There is a clear political point to be drawn from this example. Besides the causal facts that the continental European is more used to flat life than cottage existence and that sites for flats were more readily available than sites for Siedlungen, the district mayors plainly regarded the building of the sublimely impressive superblocks as a superior form of political window-dressing to the apparently piecemeal development of housing estates which were often placed beyond the city's walls and therefore were not directly reflective of virtuous local government.

However, the most important ideological associations of the Viennese superblocks, and in particular the Karl-Marx-Hof, did not derive from the expediency of local politics but from the sad episodes of the 1934 Austrian Civil War.

The events which made the superblocks the symbol of working class insurrection were described in Julius Schneider's book *Der Fall der Roten Festungen* (*The Fall of the Red Fortresses*) (Vienna, 1934) and are here described in an extract from *International Press Correspondence* which tells of the workers' resistance to Dollfuss's coup and their conversion of the Karl-Marx-Hof into a fortress:

[The flats] . . . were really citadels, but not because, as Dollfuss in his inane attempt to justify the brutal massacre of defenceless women and children maintained, that these houses, which had been planned by bourgeois architects, had been built to serve as 'armed fortresses'. They were strong fortresses because the workers defended them with their fists, with their breasts, with their last drop of blood. For three days the attacks of the government troops, who were armed to the teeth, broke against the iron resistance of the Vienna proletariat. It was only after 13 hours of preparatory artillery fire that they were able to capture the workers' premises in Ottakring. The besieged workers succeeded in retiring in good order, taking their weapons with them. . . . On the Thursday evening, after the government had twice triumphantly announced the capture of the Karl-Marx-Hof, which was bombarded with heavy howitzers planted on the heights of the Hohe Warte opposite, the police station situated in the Heiligenstadt railway station of the Franzjosefs railway was captured by the workers under cover of machine gun fire from the Karl-Marx-Hof.

(*International Press Correspondence*, No. 14, p. 142)

Figure 19 Dollfuss gives pardon with the hangman's rope, cartoon, 1934 (The Daily Worker)

Fig. 19 shows how much the workers' revolution and take-over of the Karl-Marx-Hof influenced popular taste in England; the *Daily Worker's* cartoonist, relying one presumes on agency wires, has depicted the machine-guns firing from the windows on to Dollfuss and the *Heimwehr*. No wonder that, in 1936, conservatives like H. Ingham Ashworth were anxious about the implications of flat building!

News of the revolt spread quickly: on Wednesday, 14 February 1934, *The Daily Worker* screamed the headline

AUSTRIAN WORKERS' HEROIC FIGHT
Stubborn Stand Against
Fascist Forces
Artillery Smashes Famous Vienna Model Flats

As the photographs [**Plates 68–69**] show the appearance and monumentality of the flats were well suited to the workers' siege—even if the structure was not, for after the bombardments a part of a Karl-Marx-Hof central tower collapsed. *The Daily Worker* continued:

In Vienna the Fascist troops were pounding the famous Karl Marx model flats (built by the socialist municipal council) to

pieces with artillery, in the effort to squash the workers' resistance.
(*The Daily Worker*, 14 February 1934, p. 1)

Following Breitner's fall and in resistance to Dollfuss's *Heimwehr* 5,000 men, women and children had holed themselves up in the flats and it was unsurprising that the Heimwehr did not stand back and accept the insurrection. The artillery, of course, proved too much for the workers who had, nevertheless, been provided with automatic weapons by the Communist Party. The workers were forced to evacuate the block on the night of Wednesday, 14 February, but managed to retake the building on Thursday morning. *The Daily Worker* reported that:

The first indication of the reoccupation of the Karl-Marx-Hof flats was when a machine-gun mowed down a military patrol in the streets.
(*The Daily Worker*, Friday, 16 February 1934, p. 1)

Having by these violent means drawn attention to themselves the workers' resistance was only short-lived and by Saturday of the same week *The Daily Worker* was able to publish a photograph of the chemist's shop in the Karl-Marx-Hof showing the pock marks of machine-gun bullets and the damage caused by the artillery pounding.

It was not by mere accident, then, that the unmistakable form of Ehn's Karl-Marx-Hof with its impressive kilometre-long frontages began to take on the associations of left-wing politics; not only in the armed resistance to a fascist rising but also in its very ideology (the Vienna flats had been in direct competition with private enterprise) the superblock absorbed all the associations of empirical social planning. The form, if not quite the same sort of idealism, found its second home in England in Lancelot Keay's St Andrew's Gardens, Liverpool [**Plates 83–88**], R. A. H. Livett's Kennet House, Manchester [**Fig. 125**], and the same architect's famous Quarry Hill Estate at Leeds [**Plates 71–73**]. It is probably not unconnected with this episode that the monumental Viennese style, so clearly imitated in Liverpool, never became universally popular in England. The more conservative cottage-like style of flat as practised by Louis de Soissions and at Liverpool's Speke Estate perhaps seemed ideologically and associationally safer.

Of course, the Viennese superblocks were in no way advanced in the Le Corbusier sense of the word. Their importance to the progress of flat building in Europe was as a symbol of the achievement of architecture wedded to social purpose. There were, however, at the same time other far more aesthetically advanced schemes being developed in France which while being similarly influential were more pleasing to the eye than the Karl-Marx-Hof and not one wit less sociologically sound. The most famous of these was the Cité de la Muette at Drancy, a sophisticated scheme in the International Style, which we have already had cause to discuss when mentioning the Garchey and Mopin systems of waste disposal and construction.

The Cité de la Muette, Drancy

Beaudoin and Lods essayed their Drancy scheme with a pilot project between 1930 and 1933, the Cité du Champs des Oiseaux, Bagneux. Here, in the blocks built for the Pax Society, Beaudoin and Lods also used the Mopin system of large panel construction (Mopin was himself the consulting engineer). One thousand dwellings were planned for a population of 2,971 at a density of 127 people to the acre. Unlike Drancy, there were to be no towers at the Cité du Champs des Oiseaux: the scheme was to provide for ranges of four-storey blocks with semi-basements.

The Cité de la Muette [**Figs. 20** and **22–23**] was conceived as a totally designed environment providing one-, two- and

Figure 20 Eugène Beaudoin and Marcel Lods, the Cité de la Muette, Drancy, 1934, general view

Figure 21 W. A. Eden, project for a block of flats

three-room flats for 3,900 workers and their families in a self-contained community where the triumphs of modern architecture and planning meant that the population would want for nothing. The density, at 130 people to the acre, was almost exactly the same as at Bagneux but the use of tall tower blocks enabled a smaller amount of the site to be built upon. Drancy, like Brinkmann and van der Vlught's Bergpolder Flats at Rotterdam created the European prototype of the slab block. Certainly, Drancy was a Utopian scheme: the architects planned to build 1,200 flats on their twenty-seven acre site and calculated on the basis of the built area (66,112 ft²) the density achieved was an astounding 190 people to the acre.

In *The Modern Flat* Yorke and Gibberd sensed the Utopianism of the Beaudoin and Lods scheme. They published an extremely evocative photograph [**Fig. 20** of the five tower blocks, the most eyecatching part of the scheme, taken from a specially low angle so that fronds of Drancy flora dangled delicately in focus in the foreground of the photograph contrasting with the new concrete Cité in the background, but tacitly suggesting that the new architecture could live hand-in-hand with nature.

Figure 22 Eugène Beaudoin and Marcel Lods, the Cité de la Muette, Drancy, 1934, section of a tower

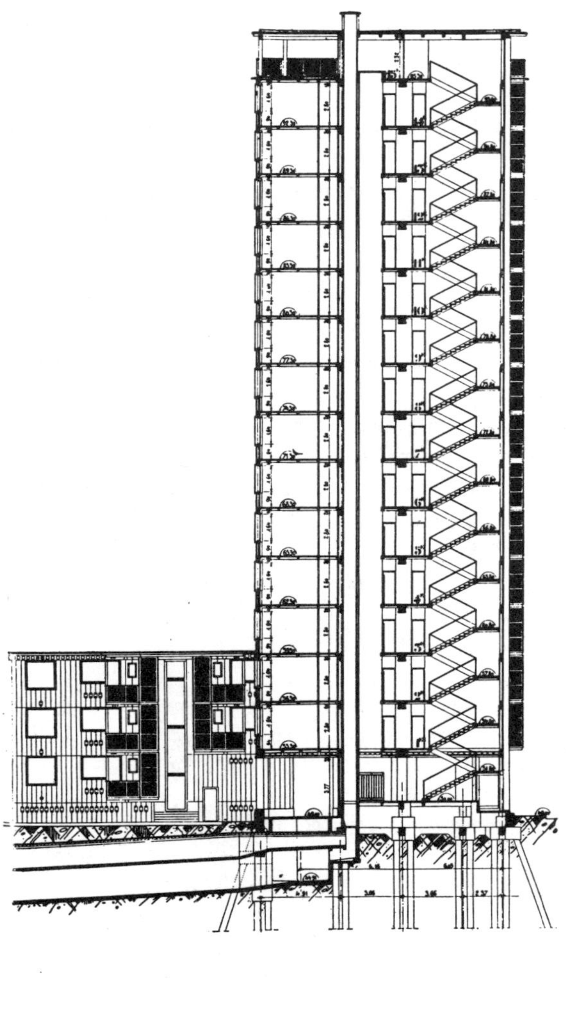

Yorke and Gibberd must have been pleased to find so suitable a real equation of tower blocks in the country; the Cité de la Muette compared very favourably with the scheme projected by W. A. Eden which they illustrated in an artist's impression at the beginning of their book [**Fig. 21** and see Appendix].

The site of the Cité de la Muette was a parallel strip of land running north-west to south-east between the Chemin de la Muette and the Route No. 30. Its layout was ordered but irregular. The central formal feature was the range of the five fifteen-storey towers which stood along the main axis of the site. North of them was a range of three-storey blocks and to their south another, larger range of three-storey flats. On the west of the site was the expected community apparatus: a church, markets, social centre and schools which all surround a large reacreation centre which had at its south-east corner the heating and refuse disposal plant of the Garchey system.

The scheme was finance under the Loucheur Law System with 10% supplied by the Public Dwelling Office of the Seine Department and 90% supplied by low-interest loans from the State. You can see that both in Austria and France, 'pioneer' housing schemes had to be funded by charitable governments: they were rarely thought to be going concerns in their own right.

The two most interesting aspects of the Cité were its use of the Mopin and Garchey systems which it did much to publicize.

Fig. 22 shows a section through a tower at Drancy and illustrates the service passages under the road used for the removal of the waste from the Garchey system.

Access to the individual flats at Drancy, whether in the towers or in the three-storey blocks, was direct by stairs and lifts. In the towers it was direct grouped; in the three-storey blocks, direct in pairs. Between each long parallel block of the three-storey flats there ran a service road. All habitable rooms were intended to overlook gardens and the towers are at the north end of each road so that no shadows would be cast over the living quarters in the lower blocks.

Such an enlightened scheme, which is at the same time so aesthetically satisfying, built with every convenience available at the given budget and with the most modern materials would, one imagines, meet with nothing less than universal approbation.

Certainly, the Cité de la Muette had a reputation: it was the source of many architectural pilgrimages including that of R. A. H. Livett who went there to study the application of the Mopin System. However, I have used the past tense throughout this description because Beaudoin and Lods's beautiful city was never completed according to their specification and for political reasons it was left unoccupied for a number of years.

Figure 23 Eugène Beaudoin and Marcel Lods, the Cité de la Muette, Drancy, 1934, plan of a tower

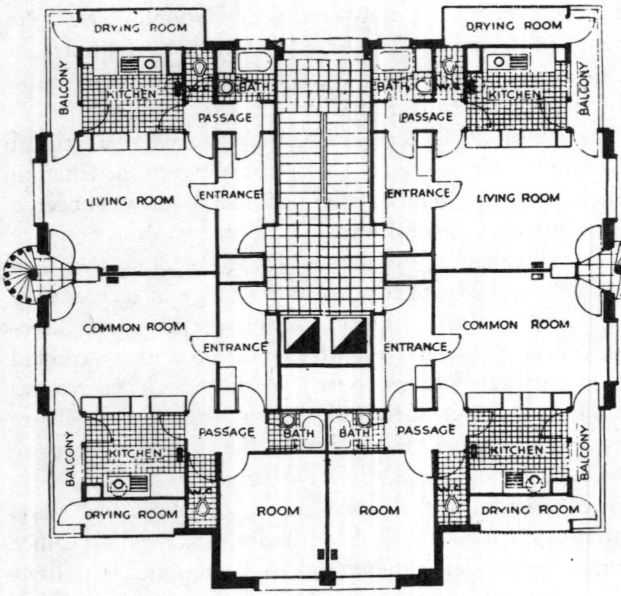

In its drab history the Cité has been used to house prisoners of war and political prisoners, and served as a transit camp for the Jewish internees of the Nazis. A weird political irony has meant that this idealistically conceived working man's city, this most utopian of planning schemes, has now become the home of the French para-military riot police!

The disillusioned Lods, the sole surviving architect, wrote in 1968 to survey the changes which time had made to his Cité:

Practically, one can say that at no time since its creation has it been used for the purpose for which it was conceived. . . . All the aspirations which Beaudoin and I had in creating it have been destroyed.

(Cited in Alison Ravetz, *Model Estate*, Croom Helm, 1974, p. 67, n. 11 trans. Stephen Bayley)

Thus was the havoc which time wrought on at least one of the modernist planned communities.

3 The CIAM congress of 1929 and the concept of minimal existence

Three strains can be detected in the influence on British flat design in the thirties. The first is the LCC's tradition of tenement building: the second is the example set by the idealistic continental model estates like the Karl-Marx-Hof in Vienna and the Cité de la Muette at Drancy near Paris, and the third is the theoretical bedrock of the movement laid down by the CIAM whose influence in England was directly through the MARS (Modern Architecture Reasearch) group. (See *Form and Function*, Part 4, No. 103).

The CIAM aimed to set down the minimum requirements for working-class living and to describe how these requirements could be attained by the intelligent application of the theory and science of modern architecture.

This achievement had to be attempted against a background in England of debate over the advantages and disadvantages of flat life which had been brought about largely by the massive decanted population waiting to be rehoused after the effects of the 1930 Slum Clearance Act.

The advantages of the flat were not immediately clear even to its proponents. *The Times* of 20 November 1936 reported a paper given by Elizabeth Denby (who had been on the design committee of Maxwell Fry's Kensal House) at the RIBA. In this paper Denby explained the contemporary attitudes of the housing debate:

Isolation, loneliness, boredom, expense in the cottage estates.

(*The Times*, 20 November 1936, p. 9c)

while in the flats:

Lack of privacy, noise, inconvenience and a barrack atmosphere.

(*Ibid.*)

Denby thought that

The general working-class opinion seemed to be that the blocks of flats would be all very well for people who could afford to send their children to boarding school, and go off themselves by car for the week-end and for holidays, but that they were definitely inadequate for families whose lives must centre in and around the home.

(*Ibid.*)

Denby's summary solution was that only by providing new flats with the community apparatus (as the Kensal House committee had done) could working-class life reach the necessary standards. The European example already existed at Drancy and at Siemensstadt (see W. Gropius, *Form and Function*, No. 96).

Maxwell Fry himself criticized the very idea of the flat when, the year after Elizabeth Denby's RIBA paper, he spoke at a DIA conference at the De la Warr Pavilion, Bexhill, where he had said that

Flat life as known in London failed to recognise the existence of children and denied the proper entry of sun and air. To live in boxes lifted off the ground and away from contact with the earth was not the life of a freeman.

(*The Times*, Monday 27 September 1937, p. 19g)

A strange attitude, indeed, for the architect of one of London's most well-known flatted developments!

There was, however, in England a campaign under way to change the image of the working-class tenement into the image of 'The Modern Flat'. Fry was, of course, part of this. There was a degree of opposition from the old men of architecture and a strong resistance to the very idea of flats among the architectural establishment. The printed discussion which followed the delivery of Grey Wornum's paper to the RIBA in 1931 had contained vociferously anti-flat attitudinizing from the pro-cottagers of the RIBA, Sir Richard Paget and Sir Theodore Chambers. Wornum's summing-up of his own paper (remember that he occupied an equivocal position in the debate) included the quotation of a passage from Anatole France's *M. Bergèret in Paris* which makes a strong contrast with the avant-garde English commentator's position *vis-à-vis* houses and the staircases cited in this unit:

And all these people who dine one above another, play piano one above another, and go to bed one above another in a perfectly symmetrical fashion, when one thinks of it, they offer a spectacle both comical and humiliating.

(Cited in *Journal of the RIBA*, 2 May 1931, pp. 438–45)

This resistance was eventually diminished by the influence of some of the prestigious flatted schemes in London and the effects of the propagandizing of the CIAM (though, one presumes, ineffectual on the ideas of Paget and Chambers) abroad and the MARS group at home. In Europe the CIAM was forced by circumstances of less sophisticated dwellings than England, and perhaps worse overcrowding, to radicalize architectural planning theory and to establish quickly the bare conditions which they could provide for workers. The pressures of rehousing made them careless of nice debates over taxonomy or questioning of rationale: the CIAM was forced to adopt a radical philosophy which became known as *Existenzminimum* (Minimal Living).

The Existenzminimum philosophy was established at the CIAM's 2nd Congress at Frankfurt in 1929 and included papers from many of the most influential architects of the day.

Ernst May delivered a paper called 'Die Wohnung für das Existenzminimum' (see *Form and Function*, Part 4, No. 106) in which he made clear his position as a supporter of the campaign for the provision of decent accommodation for the lowest income groups. It is now a commonplace (such has been the success of housing policy rhetoric) that the working man should expect to have a decent, modest dwelling and not a rat-infested, damp tenement but this commonplace was by no means clearly established in the 1930s. By means of a necessary increase in the rents charged, May believed that he had his colleagues could provide decent accommodation:

Give us dwellings, however small, but healthy and habitable, and, before all, make the rent bearable.

(*Dwellings for Lowest Income*, Hoffman, Stuttgart, 1933, p. v)

May, a socialist, said that it was because of high interest rates that private development was becoming impossible. (The German interest rate in 1929 was 11.5%!) and that, despite rationalization by the private landlords and builders, rents had increased fourfold since the pre-War period.

May's solution to the accommodation problem was one of empirical social planning:

Public bodies will therefore have to organise housing of the living income earner or there will be the danger that the financial measures, which the Government will have to take, will not ensure to the exclusive benefit of those for whom they are meant Seeing that the money for the necessary reduction of rent comes from the pocket of the public, it should, as a rule, exclusively feed public or public utility building, perhaps also one-family house construction. At no event should it be applied to the revival of speculative house-building.

(*Ibid.*, pp. v–vi)

May's attitude to the Existenzminimum philosophy was not purely one of financial rationalism but also of organic necessity. He further wrote:

Exact observation of the biological and sociological condition of the human beings that come into account for dwellings for the living income earner will keep us free from useless theories and will gradually lead us to our goal, that is the construction of dwellings just satisfying the material and mental needs of their occupants at a bearable rent.

(*Ibid.*, p. vii)

The paper given by Le Corbusier and Pierre Jeanneret, 'Analyse des élements fondamentaux du probleme de la "Maison Minimum" ' (Analysis of the Fundamental Elements of the Existenzminimum Dwelling) was more purely architectural in character than was May's.

They saw the problem as a search for new methods of approach to the housing question which by clear, rational planning would allow architects to use standardized, mass-produced components to achieve an economical, modest dwelling. But they too had a biological attitude:

The uses of the house consists in a regular sequence of definite functions. The regular sequence of these functions is a traffic phenomenon. To render that traffic exact, economical, and rapid, is the key effort of modern architectural science.

(*Ibid.*, p. ii)

The actual framework which the cousins saw for the enactment of their biological rules was a skeleton structure with 'free plan and free façades' using iron and reinforced concrete. They met any possible criticism of the expense involved with these materials before it even started by quickly asserting that if this appeared to be uneconomical it was not a fault of the materials or the architects but, rather because of a 'defective period' in industrial organization. A new approach to industry and building would create, they thought, a new architecture and a new world. Their constructional system which would also use polotis, advantageous because they took up only 0.5% of available ground space, as well as the iron and concrete could not only be applied to the Existenzminimum dwelling but it would

Allow us to face all architectural problems, from the Minimum House to the apartment house, the office building, the skyscraper, the palace . . . *if this word does not jar upon your ears.* (my italics)

(*Ibid.*, p. iv)

In comparison to the revolutionary sentiments expressed by Le Corbusier and Jeanneret, Walter Gropius delivered a dry, dull and uninspiring paper called 'Die soziologischen Grundlagen der Minimalwohnung für die städtische Bevölkerung' (The sociological foundations of minimum housing for urban populations). Gropius saw the necessity of the CIAM in establishing the Existenzminimum philosophy as:

1 To prevent the wastage of public money and to make funds available for erection of Existenzminimum buildings whose dimensions, etc., should be established by the finance 'available.

2 To reduce erection charges by spreading the costs over all categories of building.

3 To supply building land for Existenzminimum projects by confiscating the property of real estate speculators. and

4 To facilitate adventurous planning by easing of urban building regulations.

Gropius' solution in architectural terms was to build high[1] but he was never given the opportunity to realize the full extent of his vision in Germany and, instead directed his energies to designing prefabricated copper houses for the Hirsch Kupfer und Messingwerke AG of Berlin (1931).

All the propagandizing and theorizing and dreaming of the CIAM aside, a rival attraction, besides the less socially aware Stockholm International Exhibition of 1930, was the exhibition of the Deutsche Bauausstellung at Berlin in 1931.[2]

Their exhibition, called 'Housing for Our Time' gave a practical demonstration of what modern architecture and design could achieve when they were applied to the solution of the problem of creating the design-integrated living space. These experiments were not of blocks of flats to show radical new design or style but were exercises in interior design intended to maximize the utility of available space. Heinz Rau and Heinrich Schafer exhibited a student's study room with built-in wardrobes, three-light metal casement windows, divan bed, and built-in desk/drawing board. Ludwig Hilberseimer showed a more prosperous and ambitious room layout for a larger block of flats as did Otto Haeseler and Karl Völker, but the most interesting scheme came from the Berlin architect, Carl Fieger, who demonstrated that within a space of 40 m² a real Existenzminimum condition could be achieved [**Fig. 24**]. Fieger incorporated a whole range of different functions into one room. *This* was the correct direction for Existenzminimum philosophy and not the blusterings of a self-styled avant-garde of superannuated geniuses. Yet no one took advantage of Fieger's lead. Certainly in England even the most ostensibly modern schemes, for instance Kensal House, were constrained within by the most conservative, even backward, of planning layouts.

Figure 24 Carl Fieger, a 40m² room

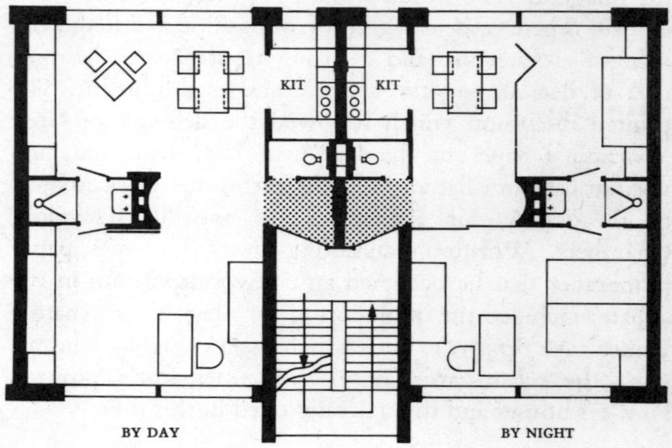

In his room Fieger showed that one small area could be altered, with the aid of screens and curtains and fold-away beds, to perform different functions by day and by night, with, depending on personal requirements, the opportunity to use the room by night for different arrangements of sleeping, breakfast and washing while by day the same room could provide separate accommodation for the requirements of living, eating and the nursery. (You should compare this with Gerrit Rietveld's ideas on flexible planning.)

Thus in 40 m² Fieger provided an adequate living accommodation for a family of four within a structurally economic space. This radical solution to the problems of the Existenzminimum was ignored by the traditional revolutionaries of architecture.

[1] Walter Gropius 'Flach-, mittel-, oder Hochbau?' in *Moderne Bauformen*, vol. 30, 1931, pp. 321–8.

[2] See *Moderne Bauformen*, vol. 30, 1931, pp. 329–47.

Part three Flats in England between the wars

Quarry Hill, Leeds

Although by no means historically the first large blocks of flats to be designed and built in England, R. A. H. Livett's Quarry Hill in Leeds was the first housing scheme in this country to bring together every strand of theory, function and idealism which we have so far mentioned into a coherent whole approaching in reality the idealistic vision of the CIAM.

Although Quarry Hill has created for itself something of a reputation as being a daring, communistic experiment, something akin to Ehn's Karl-Marx-Hof, it is really in the mainstream of English housing development, having grown out of the requirements of all building and housing legislation subsequent to the Tudor Walters Report of 1918. All this, however, would have counted for nothing had not Livett been inspired by an impressive sense of style, a social conscience and an informed knowledge of developments abroad.

It is difficult for us today to imagine with what excitement and enthusiasm a scheme like Quarry Hill was greeted [**Plate 71**]. The enthusiasm was not only that of an environmental determinism where the commentators expressed hopes of the improving nature which the new environment might have on the rehoused ex-slum-dwellers but also at the wonderful contrivances and services embodied in Quarry Hill, which we would today find very mundane. To recapture a little of the contemporary thrill you should read carefully the following quotation from *The Times*. The passage was written when large blocks of flats were still rare sights outside London and when the twentieth-century style was still a rarity in England. *The Times*' staff writer wrote his story under a photograph of a model of Livett's building. When you read it try to imagine the sublime feeling of scale which the writer was trying to suggest by exotic allusion and crisp sounding statistics:

> The site at Quarry Hill has already been cleared, and it is hoped that the whole scheme will be completed in 20 months. The flats will form part of Leeds City Council's £14,500,000 scheme to rehouse 30,000 slum families within 6½ years, and the Mopin system of construction adopted in Paris is being introduced to this country. Under this system concrete blocks made on the site are used throughout. . . . There are to be no common balconies, and at no point will more than two flats be entered from any one staircase landing. . . . The balconies and every living room throughout the block will face the sun. . . . A back to back range will be fitted to every flat, and all working and household operations will be provided for in the scullery. A gas griller is to be fitted in every flat in addition to the range, and there will be a separate domestic hot water supply. . . . A bathroom, with a lavatory [hand] basin in addition to the bath, is to be provided in every flat. A gas point is to be fixed by the side of each fireplace (in the living room and first bedroom) for those who desire gas heating. All fireplaces will be of the coke or coal burning type, and a gas poker will enable all fires to be lighted by gas.
>
> (*The Times*, 19 July 1935, p. 11c)

Figure 25 R. A. H. Livett, Kennet House, Manchester

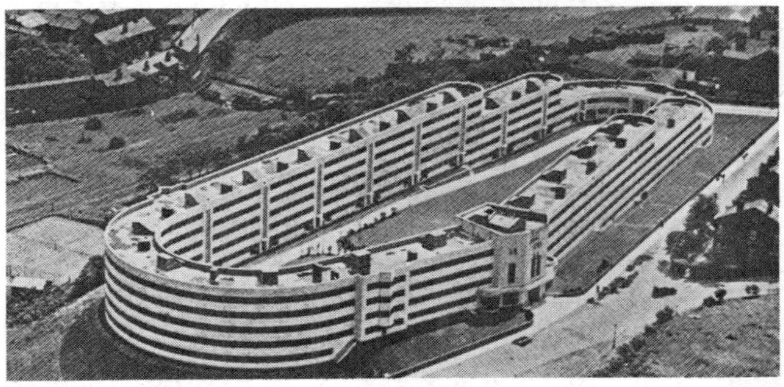

Livett became Chief Architect to the city of Leeds in 1933 and, despite his having prepared plans for large flat-blocks at Sweet Street and Kirkstall Road, the Quarry Hill flats were his single real achievement at Leeds and he undertook planning, design and supervision to a single-handed degree not usually seen in comparable schemes.

His preparation for his work in Leeds was in Manchester where, under the city architect, Leonard Heywood, he designed Kennet House in Manchester's Cheetham district [**Fig. 25**]. Kennet House, opened in 1935 when Livett was already in Leeds, can be regarded as the direct formal and ideological antecedent to Quarry Hill. Here there were curving walls describing a monumental scheme which enclosed a courtyard and embodied a physically and socially self-contained community. Besides the flats themselves, Kennet House had the usual community apparatus which we have come to expect to see in schemes of this sort, including shops, a meeting hall and a laundry. The entrance to the flats was through two imposing archways, almost an inconographic feature of 'Modern Flats'. Kennet House, alone among the traditionalist cottage-like style of Manchester housing in the 1930s struck a very modernistic note and even won contemporary acclaim from foreign visitors.

Access to the flats was by staircases within the building and, like Quarry Hill, it was planned as direct in pairs. Each flat had its own balcony and electric light and was contrived to face the sunlight. An unusual feature at this time, bearing in mind a certain resistance to the use of electricity, was the provision of an electric griller in each scullery.

The Viennese superblocks were certainly the direct formal inspitation for Livett's schemes both at Kennett House and Quarry Hill. Features like the stepped higher storeys and the perimeter layout are two obvious visual examples. As for the purely aesthetic effect it seems that Livett may have used another continental example as his inspiration. A cutting from the *Manchester Guardian* found in his office showed a photograph of Mendelsohn's Schocken Store at Chemnitz, 1929.[1] (It seems likely that, if Mendelsohn were a model, then his UFA flats in Berlin might well also have been a prototype for Livett's think-

[1] Alison Ravetz, *Model Estate*, Croom Helm, 1974, p. 58.

ing.) This curved building with its articulated horizontal bands must certainly have been Livett's stylistic starting-point, for like Kennet House and Quarry Hill seen from some angles, the Schocken store looks like a stylized ocean liner with deck after deck laid in horizontal bands. The ocean liner image had, since Le Corbusier 'coined' the metaphor, occurred to more than one commentator on the flats of the 1930s.

Similarly, the Leeds City Architect's Department was influenced by the monumentality of the Viennese schemes although, as we have seen, the social and political conditions which formed their development were not identical. The brief to Livett was that the block should not be of less than 500 individual family dwellings and should be built to a height of four storeys.

The top two floors were to be maisonettes and the flats provided ranged in size from one to four bedrooms. Small flats for the elderly were built on the ground floor. The other two straightforward requirements which the Leeds City Council made were that the flats should be self-contained and should provide individual bathrooms and lavatories. The provision of the last two items had, in any case, been mandatory since 1919 but apart from the final requirements that a central laundry be provided and only 25% of the available site be built upon Livett had a clean piece of paper with which to start. His design eventually covered only 14% of the site but only 59% was available for recreation because 27% of the area was taken up by roads.

To aid his ambitious vision's realization, Livett decided to adopt the Mopin system of large panel building. Mopin himself was interested in getting a foreign contract for his invention and it was a happy meeting when Livett was attracted by the system's simplicity and economy (it was estimated that Mopin's system was up to 15–20% cheaper than comparable ones). One unidealistic factor which may, however, have affected his decision, was that Livett was convinced that neither enough bricks nor enough bricklayers would be available in Leeds for such a large project. Similarly, Livett and his mentor, Jenkinson, must have been pleased that their new system carried the pioneering associations which they felt was appropriate to Leeds' socialist housing policy.

The system shocked England where the building techniques were hampered both by strict safety regulations and restrictive union practices, and, for instance, the Mopin system, although patently safe, did not actually meet the British fire resistance standards and Livett only with difficulty had his design approved.

If Livett had followed the dictum to build only to four storeys, as the Leeds City Council had laid down in their brief, its total provision of accommodation would not have matched Jenkinson's and Livett's vision. It was only with the ultimate increase to eight storeys and the inevitable inclusion of lifts (which had not originally been part of the specification) that the 938 total flats were built.

The Tudor Walters Report had expressed fear that a large scullery in working-class housing would encourage the abandonment of the living room which would be left as a show-piece 'parlour'. Livett did not have enough space to play with to constitute such a risk for at Quarry Hill the scullery was forced into a position between the bathroom and the living room (a legacy of the period when the bath and scullery were one) and the door opened out on to a cramped balcony which was, despite the attendant propaganda, in fact good for nothing except the entry to the coal-hole [**Fig. 26**].

Figure 26 R. A. H. Livett, Quarry Hill, Leeds, 1934–41, plan of typical rooms

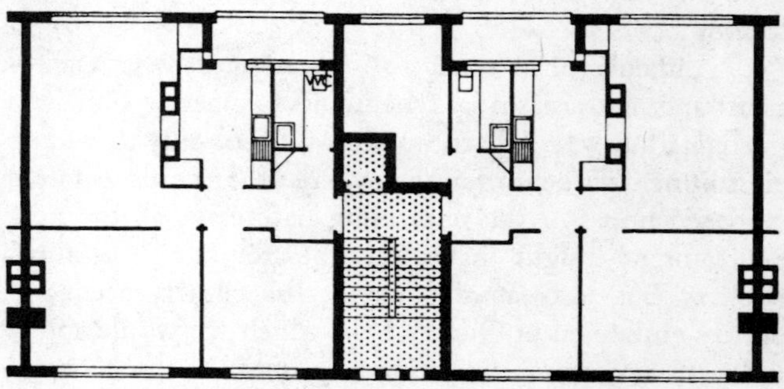

However, Livett did lavish some care in the scullery and included for his residents a deep sink and the Garchey system of waste disposal. Livett's flats have been renovated once and because of the massively increasing costs of maintenance and the new policy of depopulating the central urban area they are to be demolished.

Kensal House, Ladbroke Grove

Kensal House which has already been mentioned in Units 17–18, was built by one of the housing associations which were active in the field of flat design in the 1930s. A committee of architects including Maxwell Fry, Elizabeth Denby, Robert Atkinson, C. H. James and Grey Wornum was responsible for its conception and design (film strip frame 8).

Kensal House, which was built in 1937, was sponsored by the Gas Light and Coke Company Ltd. and was an attempt to provide for working men modern accommodation in a variety of different sizes. Its principal architect, Maxwell Fry, considered that Kensal House embodied the benefits of both technical and social experimentation. Of it he said:

> Unless technical advance is made to contribute directly to increasing the total of human happiness it is largely wasted.
> (E. Maxwell Fry, 'Kensal House' in *Ascot* . . . 1938, pp. 56–60)

Fry's brief was to design the perfect setting for an English type of *Existenzminimum* and to do so he decided to rely on the application of technology to building design. This conscious attitude, very much derived from the CIAM philosophy, was new to England.

Fry was, however, aware of the paradox that while mass-production made cheaply available advanced building techniques and machines like the Ascot water heater, by its very nature it dehumanized the working man and caused problems all of its own. It was Fry's opinion that Kensal House went some way towards solving the problems caused by the division of labour [**Plates 70–79**].

Like an industrialist, Fry multiplied one basic unit of accommodation around the site. On the ground floor the flats had two bedrooms (because space had to be allowed for entrance halls and stair-wells) while everywhere else they had three or four bedrooms. The access was direct in pairs and the individual flat plan was one of extreme simplicity. The front door opened into a hall with the bathroom/WC and kitchen (sharing the central service core) immediately on the right or the left, the living room straight ahead, and on the side of the hall opposite the services were arranged the three bedrooms. One quirk of the plan was that the door of the master bedroom opened out into the living room and not into the hall.

Fry was against gallery access because it militated against the sense of privacy essential to his conception of the Kensal House urban village. The bedrooms were all designed small to maximize on space in the living quarters and it was the same ergonomic interest which made Fry design the kitchen along functional lines. On one wall were the sink and draining boards and the copper; on the other the shelves and the table. The cooker was placed at the end of the working surface. More working surface was supplied under the light of the window while the largest working table was supplied with a gas point for the gas iron.

Six pram and cycle sheds were under cover in each main stair entrance and twelve were supplied under the galley of the west block. The social club occupied the ground, floor of the east block.

You can see in **Plate 79** how Fry wilfully used the 4 in. reinforced concrete to make purely decorative shapes in the entrance and covered way.

The finishes included cork-lined walls within and concrete paint without; the floors were of a patent tile and concrete construction which was covered throughout with 'battleship linoleum' cemented to the floor.

The innovations at Kensal House were not so much in structure or systems as in the special character given to the estate by the carefully considered community apparatus, the club and the nursery. In this, the influence of the 1930 *Slum Clearance Act* had been a strong one and the committee felt a strong conviction to provide precisely what it believed the ex-slum-dwellers to have lacked.

According to Elizabeth Denby the committee's brief was

> To comply with national and local regulations and requirements, to design an estate suitable for a comparatively mixed but poor population, with large families, and to see that the weekly outgoings on fuel and light were as reasonable as the rents.
>
> (E. Denby 'Kensal House, An Urban Village', *Ascot*, 1938, pp. 61–4)

Denby believed that the clubs would be an improving influence on the residents. This kind of physical determinism has now become a little dated but, nevertheless, in 1938 it was possible to write:

> It is like a conjuring trick to see how infants entering at two years of age with the expression of men who have been through Borstal and Wormwood Scrubs, are in a couple of months transformed into carefree, happy babies.
>
> (*Ibid.*, p. 62)

The designing committee was consciously anxious to encourage a village atmosphere and village associations. Workshops were included in the clubs and, continuing the mythology of the International Style,

> On a sunny evening or at the week-end each balcony has its tenants leaning elbows on the rail, smoking, gossiping, happy, like a group of cottagers perched above each other on a steep cliff. The possession of canaries by some of the tenants intensifies the country illusion.

It is a curious paradox that one of London's most noteworthy Modern Movement flat buildings should have its originators talking in terms which might more easily be expected to come from the exponents of Garden City philosophy!

The tenants of Kensal House were poor to very poor, being rehoused slum dwellers. After paying rent it was calculated that each family had on average 3s–3s 6d a week to spend on food and clothing per head but, despite this poverty, the new residents were 'aglow with pride at their new homes'[1] and were thought to be examples of the potentialities in slum dwellers which good modern architecture could release.

Kensal House and Quarry Hill were two exceptional working-class housing schemes of the 1930s. Before we continue to contrast two further working-class flat blocks. Lancelot Keay's modernistic St Andrew's Gardens, Liverpool, with Connell, Ward and Lucas's modern Kent House, Kentish Town, I want you to consider briefly two middle-class flatted developments of the 1930s.

[1] Denvy, E., in *Flats*, Ascot Gas Water Company Ltd., London, 1938, p. 63.

Ellington Court, Southgate

Ellington Court, Southgate, was built by Frederick Gibberd in 1937. Gibberd was the co-author, with F. R. S. Yorke, of *The Modern Flat*, so we can fairly assume that at Ellington Court, Gibberd applied all the principles of the science of flat building to his modest solution to the needs of middle-class housing in a London suburb (film strip frame 7).

We must consider, together with Ellington Court, Minoprio and Spenceley's Fairacres at Roehampton, another middle-class development (see pp. 00–00). Considered together they make a nice contrast with the working-class schemes described here not only because they were designed and built for people with different tastes, and expectation, but also because the higher rents which could be charged (a three-room flat at Ellington Court would cost up to £2 8s 0d a week compared with 9s 6d at Kensal House) enabled the architect to seek a refinement of design, structure and site not possible in low rent properties. Here, the ideal—we must assume—was nearly possible.

The high rents enabled the architects to use more expensive facing materials. Both Ellington Court and Fairacres use brick, a material considered more attractive and more associationally pure for façade work than concrete.

The site of Fairacres overlooks Roehampton Golf Course, and Ellington Court was built on the site of an older house, placed well back from Southgate High Street, where the mature grounds, planting and tennis courts (now no longer there) were preserved for the new tenants.

Gibberd's brief was to provide for the professional and business classes three- and four-bedroom family flats. His style for the job was not reductive but full of finesse and with the simplest of ingredients—brick, metal casement windows, concrete balconies and floors—Gibberd created a group of buildings of undeniable visual dignity and with a marked air of quality **[Plates 80–82]**.

His plan was of a staggered T shape with lawns and garages on one side and the gardens on the other **[Fig. 27]**. Access to the flats was the usual system for blocks of this size, being direct in pairs and so clearly articulated are the internal divisions of Gibberd's plan that the flats are almost only one remove away from single-family dwelling houses.

Certainly, at Ellington Court Gibberd had plenty of space to play with for his completed scheme covered 60,548 ft.² and only 17.5% of this was built on, giving a low density of twenty-six flats to the acre. Thus the population density of about eighty people to the acre was extremely low for a flatted scheme. Two of the blocks had two flats per floor; two other blocks had four flats per floor. Each block was of three storeys and there were thirty-six in total with provision for the caretaker being made on the roof.

Curiously, even in this middle-class scheme Gibberd thought it appropriate to build a communal lounge for the residents. There were, however, no workshops or nurseries but rather ten lock-up garages were provided (not as high a ratio as Fairacres but remember that at Kensal House and Quarry Hill residents were meant to keep their bicycles in the pram store and no provisions whatsoever was made for cars) and the original tennis court was retained.

The mechanical services included at Ellington Court were the central heating and hot-water plant, located in the basement, and the 'Thermidair' convector heating units. A coal fire was provided for aesthetic purposes and there was an electric socket provided for fires in the bedrooms and a point for an electric cooker in the kitchen. Constant hot water was supplied to the bath, hand-basin and sink. Hot water was also used to warm the linen cupboard.

Gibberd used a rather unusual method of construction at Ellington Court. The building was based on a series of 9 in. parallel brick cross walls which had the metal windows placed in their ends **[Fig. 28]**.

Figure 27 Frederick Gibberd, Ellington Court, Southgate, 1936, plan

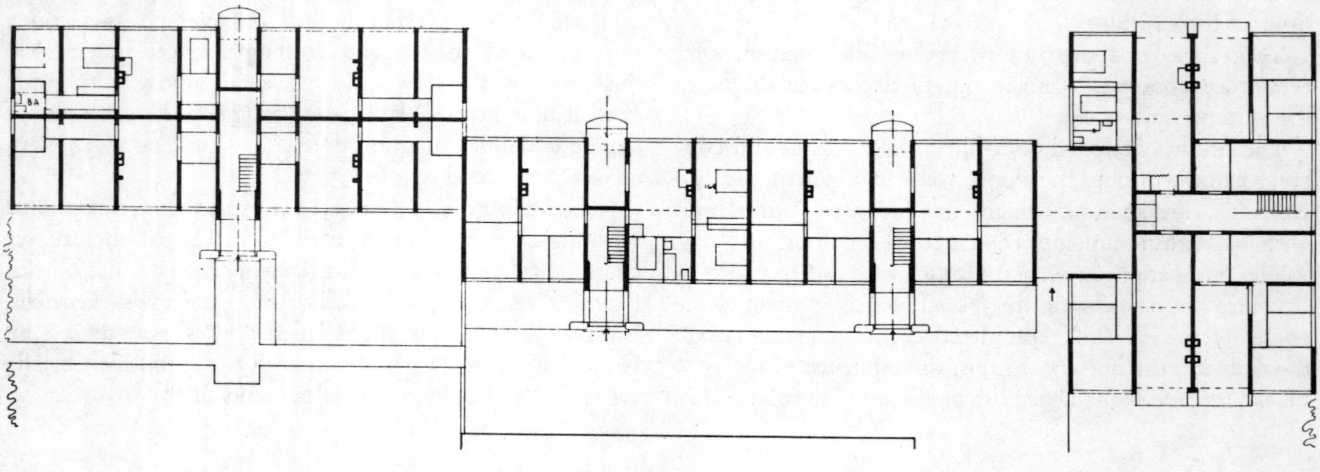

Figure 28 Frederick Gibberd, Ellington Court, Southgate, 1936, isometric view showing system of construction

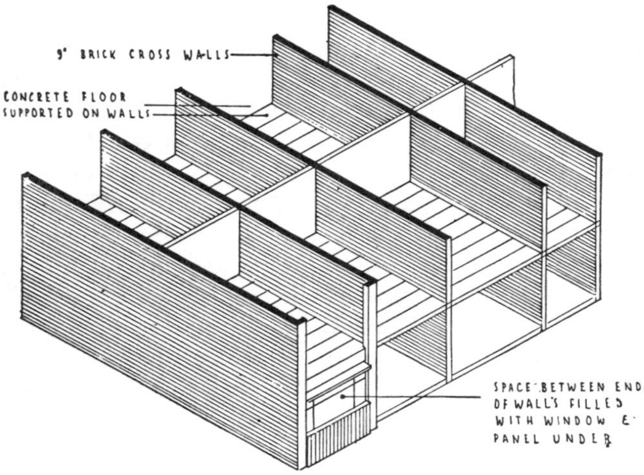

Because the brick cross walls together with the reinforced concrete floors which spanned the whole building provided the main load-bearing members Gibberd could allow himself free decorative play with the end walls which, to emphasize their non-structural nature, are made up out of vertically-laid bricks. The flat roof was covered with three-ply bituminous felt.

Because this expensive but simple constructional system required no beams or internal members Gibberd was able to have completely simple, square-ended rooms with full-width windows providing the spacious, light and airy interiors which he and Yorke had considered so essential to the aesthetic effect of the modern flat.

Plate 54 shows the utilitarian simplicity which the architect sought to achieve in his interiors. The internal folding doors could be opened out to enlarge the amount of available space and, for entertaining, the dining recess could similarly be extended on to the balcony.

What are the essential differences between Kensal House and Ellington Court?

• You can see from this brief description that effectively the standard of accommodation offered in a middle-class flat differed little from that of a working-class one. The principal difference, besides the greater size, was the use of more expensive finishes and, secondarily, the more expensive site and setting. •

Fairacres, Roehampton Lane

The general plan of Fairacres, a luxury scheme of flats in south-west London, was to provide sixty-four flats on a site of six acres. The plan chosen by the architects, Minoprio and Spenceley, was of an arc so that each flat could take advantage of the site's most important asset: the fine views over Roehampton golf course. For this luxury scheme it was considered essential that road traffic should be restricted to just one side of the building and because of this both service and main entrance shared the same, outer side of the building.

Figure 29 Minoprio and Spenceley, Fairacres, Roehampton, 1935, plan

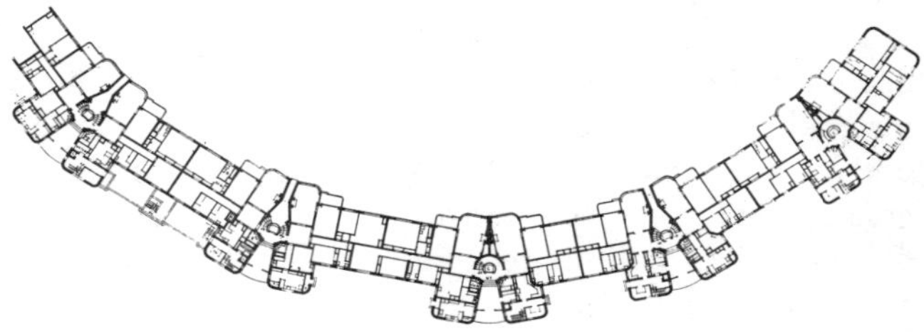

The plan was of four storey blocks divided into eight distinct units [**Fig. 29**].

Each block contained eight flats served by a lift and two staircases. The individual flats were L-shaped with the front door, which faced the stair well, centrally placed. A typical four-bedroom flat had three bathrooms, dressing room, dining room, drawing room, kitchen with dining recess and a balcony. There was a service lift to the kitchen and one of the bedrooms was for a maid. If you compare this plan [**Fig. 30**] with the plan of Ediwn T. Hall's Sloane Mansions you might see some marked similarities [**Plate 56**].

The eight principal entrances were placed between each of the projecting wings. From the entrance the resident could choose to ascend either in a lift or up a circular stair well. Inside the flat there is no evidence of the curvature of the building because the roundness is taken up by the service area and the entrance halls.

The internal functional divisions of the flat are clearly marked. Sleeping, living and service areas are strictly delineated.

Figure 30 Minoprio and Spenceley, Fairacres, Roehampton, 1935, flat plan

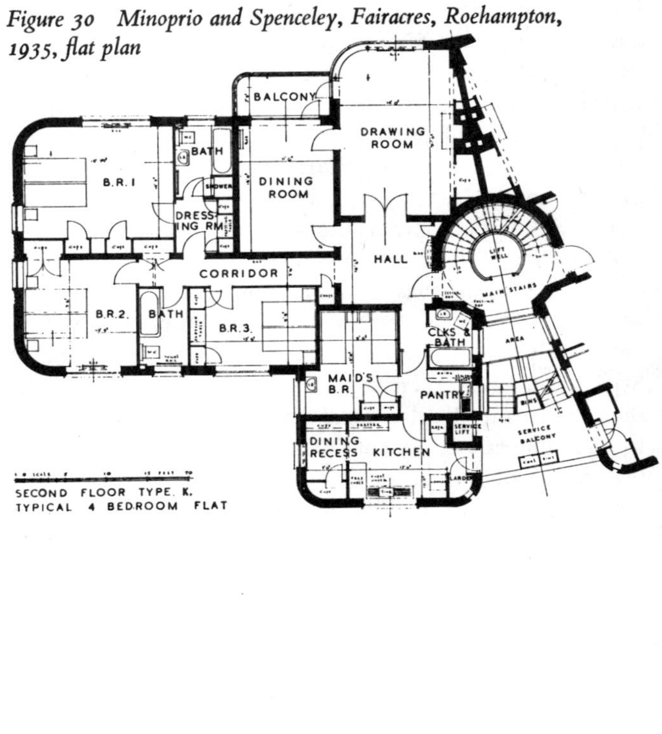

The architects also provided fitted furniture and the entrance to the dining room even had a built-in loudspeaker over the door.

The construction was of solid brick walls, chosen because brick transmits less noise than any other building material and the high rents could defray initial capital outlay. Noise and its extinction was a prime concern of the architects at Roehampton and they devised a new method of flooring with hollow tiles surmounted by cylindrical rubber pads 1½ in. by 2 ft. on which were laid a floating floor of reinforced concrete 1½ in. thick. Similarly, the heating and water pipes were wrapped in fabric to prevent drumming and vibration.

The services provided were an automatically stoked coke-fired boiler for the central heating and hot water supply; radiators in all habitable and communication rooms; centralized refrigeration and relayed four-channel radio.

It is an indication of the income group at which Fairacres was aimed to add that the architects thought it necessary to provide no less than sixty separate garages, chauffeurs' rooms and a car repair workshop. There were two lodges to provide seven flats for the porters and other service staff.

Fairacres was Edwardian in its opulence and quite untypical of its time. It has been included here to demonstrate what could be achieved in flat design when the architects had a no-holds-barred commission. In these circumstances, a flat, as W. Shaw Sparrow, had said, was truly a substitute for a house. But do you think that the conditions provided in, say, Kensal House, adequately compensated for the Englishman's loss of his sovereign rights: his house, his home, his garden?

Comparison of St Andrew's Gardens and Kent House

We have looked at two prominent examples of working-class flats and two interesting examples of higher-income flats. I want now to compare two very different working-class housing projects as a summary to this section on the flat in England in the 1930s. The comparison is between Lancelot Keay's St Andrew's Gardens in Liverpool [**Plates 83–88**] and Connell, Ward and Lucas's Kent House, Kentish Town, London [**Plates 89–94**]. In the question of style in the 1930s they exemplify the two opposing trends, although their purpose—while on different scales—was identical (filmstrip frames 9–12).

Keay's scheme was a concessionary modernistic one with Viennese details while Connell, Ward and Lucas's flats were built in an uncompromisingly International Style idiom. Keay's estate is in what we can now see to be standard-quality English local authority flat style informed by the influence of the continent. Keay's style was not the historicism of a Louis de Soissons (Maxwell Fry had said that to a conservative Englishman only decency could be Georgian[1]) but it was an architecture which played stylistically safe and explored very different ground from that advocated by MARS architects and, in particular, Connell, Ward and Lucas.

Connell, Ward and Lucas often came up against local authority (see Broadcasting Supplement for radio programme 18 where Basil Ward talks about Connell, Ward and Lucas's difficulties with Ruislip District Council) and had experienced difficulty at Amersham with Connell's design for High and Over. The same difficulty could be expected from other local authorities and they never built for a municipality. Kent House was designed and built for the St Pancrras House Improvement Society and we must assume that local authorities found the associations of the Viennese superblocks in schemes like Keay's more easy to live with than the aesthetic revolution of MARS.

St Andrew's Garden's, Liverpool

Lancelot Keay built these flats on the old Trowbridge Street site. Because of its central circular motif [**Plate 88**] the buildings are inevitably known by their residents as 'the bullring'. Like Kensal House, St Andrew's Gardens were a direct outcome of the rehousing encouraged by the 1930 *Slum Clearance Act*, taking residents from an 'unhealthy area'.

There were four blocks in the scheme. C was begun in November 1932 and housed seventy-five flats (sixteen with two bedrooms and fifty-nine with three); block B was the next and contained forty-five flats (five two-bedroom; forty three-bedroom); this was followed by block A which had forty flats (fifteen two-bedroom and twenty-five three-bedroom) and the last to be completed was block D, the largest, having 156 flats (four one-bedroom, fory-six two-bedroom and one hundred and six three-bedroom).

The most evocative block is D, with the massive curved façade and the round arched entrances to what was once

Figure 31 Lancelot Herman Keay, St Andrew's Gardens, Liverpool, 1937, architect's impression

[1] E. Maxwell Fry, 'The Architect's Problem, cited in Ravetz, 1974, p. 137.

a tree-filled play area. Clearly, Keay had been influenced in his formalism and his details by the example of Ehn's Karl-Marx-Hof. He had even been to Austria himself[1] where he must have absorbed the influence at first hand. Block D is of five storeys with identical flats on each floor except at ground level where the stairways and entrance halls interrupt the standard pattern. The standard unit plan depends on the number of bedrooms but the common accommodation provided was living room, scullery, bathroom, hall, larder, fuel store and balcony.

Keay used gallery access. Each gallery is gained by curious, militaristic enclosed stairwells which clearly have their origins in Vienna [**Plate 86**] and any gallery which serves more than five flats is contrived in such a way that it is fed by two staircases. Only the service rooms look out into the courtyard; all the living rooms have external views. The bedrooms in all flats open directly off the hall.

Keay was influenced in his plan by the siting of the railway line and the intention to maintain the existing thoroughfares. His constructional system was to use concrete piers to go down to the solid rock; these supported reinforced concrete lintels which carried the external walls, stairs and party walls. Following the regulations, the external walls are 14 in. thick up to the height of the fourth floor and decrease to 11 in. after that. Internal constructional walls are 9 in. thick while partition walls are 4½ in. The whole ground floor is a solid concrete slab while the upper floors have reinforced concrete floors. You can see that the Liverpool authorities were anxious that their vigour to clear the slums of the city should be expressed in such a monumental way. The round arches which Keay used contrast with Livett's not in shape (for they are almost identical) but in structure: Livett's fortress used a light steel frame with concrete panels to form his arched entrances; Keay's are constructed with an almost medieval solidity.

The balconies were formed out of cantilevered reinforced concrete with fronts of 9 in. brick stiffened with reinforced concrete uprights. The stairs are made of pre-cast concrete units.

The external appearance of St Andrew's Gardens is very much dictated by the finishes employed. The main body of the building is made up of golden-brown rustic brick with darker-coloured plinths bound together with yellow mortar. The copings and dressings are of artificial stone and the windows are metal casements. (Strange to say these are now (1974) being replaced by wooden ones.) The roof tiles are 18 in. by 12 in. concrete slabs.

The total cost of St Andrew's Gardens was £133,450 giving an average cost of £422 for each of the 316 flats. The cost was, therefore, almost identical to that of Kent House in unit pricing.

The relatively high budget allowed Keay to employ a wide range of service facilities for his residents. The heating was by open fire and boiler in the living room and there was a fireplace in the master bedroom. The independent hot water system served both bath and sink being served by a hot-water cylinder with immersion heater placed behind the living-room fire.

In the kitchen there was a gas-point, sink with draining board, a larder placed off the lobby (to provide outside ventilation) and some fitted cupboards.

The WC had outside ventilation, a euphemism current in the 1930s to explain that the WC was in an exposed position, and was normally included in the bathroom except in the one-bedroom flats where it was placed separately, the bath being in the scullery.

For laundering residents were provided with a gas washing-copper. Metal holders were also provided to support washing lines projecting from the balconies.

The method of waste disposal chosen by Keay was a 15-in. stoneware chute with a hopper at each floor. One chute was to serve two or three flats per floor and the waste fed into a blue-brick-lined receptacle at ground level. There were no containers involved in this system.

Kent House, Ferdinand Street, Kentish Town

Kent House, built by Connell, Ward and Lucas for the St Pancras House Improvement Society, makes a marked contrast with Keay's St Andrew's Gardens. It is situated in a small side road off Chalk Farm Road and is not immediately more striking than the tall nineteenth-century building which stands on one side of it.

Connell, Ward and Lucas's original plan for the Kent House project (a housing scheme to provide three- and four-room working-class flats) was so efficient of space that it gave more flats on the site than the LCC allowed. The design had to be changed from the original linked blocks [**Fig. 32**] to the two separate blocks which form the present building.

Figure 32 Connell, Ward and Lucas, Kent House, Kentish Town, London, 1936, axonometric view of the original scheme

[1] See Ravetz, Sutcliff, A., ed., *Multi-storey Living*, Croom Helm, Barnes and Noble, London, 1974. p. 148, n. 16.

Besides the hard edge of MARS stylism Kent House provided another weapon *pour êpater le bourgeois*—the colour. While St Andrew's Gardens was a very sober and proper Peabody brown, heavy with the associations of philanthropy and improvement, Kent House was originally colour-washed pink with blue staircases and bright red balconies [**Plates 89–94.**]

Like Kensal House and St Andrew's Gardens, Kent House was a direct product of the 1930 *Slum Clearance Act* and it was financed by the provisions made in that act. The subsidy was used as a pool to help out the poorest families. The basic rents were 5s 6d per week per habitable room totalling out at 13s 6d for a three-roomed flat and 18s per week for a four-roomed flat.

Access to the flats was by exposed staircases [**Plate 00**] and was laid out as direct in pairs. The bathroom and kitchen, forming the central service core, were grouped together and the kitchen opened out on to the balcony. Unlike Kensal House where the master bedroom opened into the living-room no rooms at Kent House opened off one another. The balconies were cantilevered directly off the floor slab and were designed to be large enough for a table and chairs. You can see in **Fig. 32** that only half the ground area was built upon; this allowed space for storage of prams and bicycles (it is now used as an informal car port) and allowed free circulation of air. The building is supported over this free area by massive pilotis of steel with concrete poured inside them [**Plate 93**].

The building was made out of a reinforced concrete frame with the external walls acting as deep beams to carry the floors. Inside, the walls are lined with $\frac{1}{2}$-in. wall board given a thin coat of plaster. The structure of the building makes internal load-bearing walls unnecessary. The floors are finished in a jointless composition substance.

The refuse disposal is by chutes on each floor with the provision for them to be flushed from the top. The rubbish fell into an enclosed chamber and truck on the ground floor and was collected by the municipal service.

The heating at Kent House was by back-to-back grates between living room and kitchen.

The hot water from the fire in the living room was stored in a cylinder which had an immersion heater for use in summer when no fire would be in use. The kitchen was supplied with points for gas cooking and an oven was incorporated into the grate. There was a sink and draining board, a built-in larder-cupboard just off the kitchen ventilated from the balcony, and a built-in table with cupboards and drawers.

The WC was in the bathroom and all the piping was enclosed so as to provide the machine-finish unity of appearance so essential to the International Style aesthetic.

Similarly, there were built-in wardrobes in the bedrooms and while it might seem paradoxical that the machine-finish MARS block had smoky coal fires inside it, just like any nineteenth-century tenement, it might serve to emphasize the point that for all the ideological attitudinizing the International Style was as much pure formalism as any other.

Conclusion

Looking back—the achievements of the flat

Any survey of this modest length must, of course, be selective. I have chosen examples which support my argument rather than those which would give an uncritically wide conspectus of flat building in the first half of this century. Perhaps it would have been possible to choose entirely different examples to suggest a different thesis of the development of the flat in England, but what I have tried to do in the limited space available is describe the development of the three types of flat, the tenement block, the mansion-house and the modern flat. I hope that I have, at least, made it clear that the conditions and ideals of modern architecture meant that the tenement block and the mansion house block coalesced into the modern flat type in the third and fourth decades of this century. I have tried, also, to sketch the roles of legislation in housing policy, the effect of a politico-symbolic burden from the continent and the extent to which mechanical servicing and services were employed in creating the modern flat. I admit, certainly, that an alternative pattern of development could be discerned, but I feel that the events as I have described them neatly outline the evolution of the flat from the nineteenth-century tenement to its acceptance first by the upper classes and, later, by the middle classes. Responsibility for this creation of respectability lies with the theorizers of the modern movement ideology and in them, too, it found its demise.

1 Can you suggest (from the evidence I have given in this unit) what were the overall general improvements in living standards created in flats in the first half of the century?

2 What developments encouraged these improvements?

3 What progress is discernible in flat building between the wars?

● 1 We all know the prints circulated by graphic artists like Gustave Doré which illustrated the conditions of working-class housing in nineteenth-century London. Overcrowded houses, packed in at eighty or so to the acre, with privies in the back-yard and (perhaps) a single cold water tap inside. Tenements were in many cases inferior even to these horrific examples of bad housing. At least the terraced house offered cross-ventilation, that hallowed symbol for Modern Movement adoration, while in tenements scant attention was paid to anything other than the mean aim of crowding in as many people as possible into one building. By the fourth decade of the twentieth century those who were lucky enough to be the beneficiaries of the largesse of a progressive housing association or a prosperous local authority could experience life in a controlled environment within a rationally-designed flat. There would be hot and cold running water, a bathroom and a WC *inside* the flat, the heating, even if only by primitive coal fires, was readily available. There would be—no matter what the style of the flat—large areas of glass to let in Modern Movement sunshine (always more apparent in theoretical writings than in practical reality) and a hygienic balance would be maintained by the provision of cross-ventilation.

If the working poor experienced a considerable rise in living standards then, perhaps, the rich experienced a comparative decline. Comparison of the differential between a tenement and a modern working-class flat shows a much larger margin of difference than between an Edwardian mansion-house block (say, Edwin T. Hall's Sloane Mansions) and a luxury block of the 1930s (say, Minoprio and Spenceley's Fairacres) demonstrates this. In 1900 a flat for the rich could be designed with a promiscuous wastage of space high on the brief and, with coal cheap, servants plentiful and a grate in every room, could be kept warm economically, easily and constantly. The residents in a mansion-house flat probably hardly realized that they were not in a house. In comparison, Fairacres, for instance, was much less luxurious and more thrifty in its use of space and resources. It seems that a levelling-off in difference between the flats of the poor and the rich is perceptible.

2 The developments which aided this improvement were the apparent economies of high-density, tall housing ('apparent' because subsequent experience has now discredited the theory), the provision of greater internal space made possible by modern methods of construction, the use of electricity, which requires no large-scale, individual capital plant, as a method of lighting and heating, and the assumption by both local and national governments of their role as providers and legislators in housing affairs.

3 The overall progression in flat design between the wars can be described as the story of the encroachment of the International Style into England. With the International Style came the high-minded Corbusian belief in modern technology and the benefits it could bring. The change is apparent in examining the appearance of the LCC's East Hill Estate and Wells Coates's Isokon Flats in Hampstead. A mere two decades separates the two. The former as an example of a traditional architectural style in the service of the modern flat, the latter as an example of the exuberant optimism of the International Style at its most seductive and least practical. The story of the International Style in England is a sad parable of disillusion. ●

Despite some successful experiments the flat has never really caught on in England; English love of home *and* garden was to prove stronger than the persuasions of the internationalists. At the end of the 1930s the cottage-or flat debate was revived throughout Europe. The comparison with Modern Movement ideology is a telling one.

Reconsider, for a moment, Wells Coates's Isokon Flats as exemplars of Modern Movement housing ideology [**Plates 55–56**]. It was the Isokon Flats which brought the International Style *and* the modern flat to England. If not architecturally the most active exponent of the cause of the functional flat built for twentieth-century needs, Coates was, instead, perhaps the most eloquent advocate of the movement which sought to wed mass-production techniques to social purpose. Coates had been born in Japan and it is, perhaps, easier to appreciate how he could have created the shockingly severe Isokon Flats on reading the following passage:

A man whose eyes have been trained in the East will only rarely want to open them in the West. . . . Indifferent to the confusion of appearances and reappearances, the accretion of layer upon layer of architectural growth, he is able to track down its underlying shape, the source of its traditions.

(Wells Coates, 'Response to Tradition', *Architectural Review*, October 1932, pp. 165–8)

Despite this slightly mystical tone, Coates was clearly an incisive thinker. He had a functionalist's brain and, naturally, rejected all ornament. In writing of the ideal room he said

How rarely they [the last generation] were aware that a room exists for the man, and not man for the room, that he and not the bric-a-brac is to be given the best possible setting.

(Wells Coates, *Architectural Association Journal*, LIII, April 1938, p. 614)

Coates was here describing the ideal controlled environment in which he and his intellectual colleagues could flourish. This was the thinking man's *Existenzminimum*. His ideal was that of all experimentors in flat dwelling: mass-production housing and social reorganization. Looking so far into the future he overlooked anomalies in his theory and the realistic restrictions which would hamper the creation of his ideal. It is strange to think that the man who wrote

It is for architects to realise the possibilities of our lives, now, in an age of Science, when life could almost immediately become free, that is to say, ordered, and refined, for all classes. Imprisonment (with torture) in the straitjacket of old forms, a pretence to beauty at second hand? Or liberation (with refinement and delight) into movement, balance harmony, order from in outwards?

(Wells Coates, 'Inspiration from Japan', *Architects' Journal*, Nov. 1931, pp. 586–7)

and who could envisage the future with people in Isokon cells listening to their Coates-designed Ekco radios (see **Unit 20 plate 119**) would so soon witness a return to historicist, vernacular housing ideals for Coates—as did the Modern Movement throughout Europe—underestimated the strength of the ordinary man's resistance to modernism.

The same *dénouement* occurred in Austria where, in 1942, just eleven years after Coates's vision of the future was written, Dr Max Ermers, one of the consultants of the Austrian Garden Cities Association and a moving force behind the creation of the Viennese superblocks, took stock of Vienna's achievements. Unhappily for the supporters of the flat ideal, Ermers was disillusioned by the lack of social success of his superblocks. Certainly, he thought the boldness of the conception and the scale of the Viennese example a noteworthy precedent but he said that

We must confess nevertheless that not everything we tried succeeded at the first attempt and the results finally achieved were very unequal.

(Max Ermers, 'Housing Policy in Vienna', *Town & Country Planning*, Nov. 1941, p. 140)

and he regretted that Vienna had not decided to build many more single-family cottages. Those 'Siedlers' were happier people than the flat dwellers. Vienna had built nearly thirty garden suburbs to re-house almost 20,000 people. Each of the *Siedlungen* worked as a co-operative unit and their members even helped in the construction of the estates. Each resident was estimated to have contributed about 2,000 man hours to the estate. This was quite possible with the low-pitch technology used in cottages but more difficult when steel erection was required for flats.

Each of the dwellings was larger than the comparable flats and, while there were still no bathrooms in the cottager, each unit dwelling was cheaper than the flat because of offset production costs. In the *Siedlungen* planning could more freely operate and residential streets were separated from the traffic-bearing ones. Each *Siedlungen* had the usual community apparatus and

Thus with the help of the sunshine, fresh air, gardens for food and recreation and the relative spaciousness of the houses the children of the Viennese workers came to live in a hitherto undreamed of paradise.

(Ermers, *op. cit.*, p. 140)

So that was the final solution in Vienna of the battle between flat and cottage.

It is clear that the flat offers only apparent economy because the lower unit cost per dwelling has to contend with the problems of expensive regular maintenance, provision of elaborate services not necessary in cottages and the risk of vandalism—the cost of social experimentation.

We shall see in Unit 23 how the Garden City movement, the embodiment of the cottage ideal, and the exponents of the flat started off from common premises but eventually diverged into opposition while still both embracing the same philanthropic ideals.

Appendix

In preparing this unit I was fortunate to have the opportunity of meeting and talking to the distinguished architect, W. A. Eden, whose project for a block of modern flats is illustrated in **Fig. 21**. In our conversation it became clear that Mr Eden was soon disillusioned by the modernist ideology and aesthetic which his project so eloquently displays. To explain further how an architect who was at first impressed by the International Style and its housing policy became progressively less enthusiastic about its form and purpose I asked Mr Eden to contribute a short text which, with his permission, is printed below.

Humane architecture

In the mid-thirties, when the project shown in the illustration [**Fig. 21**] appeared in the *Architectural Review* in connection with a series of three articles I contributed on 'The Making of the English Landscape', the Liverpool School of Architecture was in something of a ferment. Professor Sir Charles Reilly had recently retired from the Roscoe Chair of Architecture to be succeeded by Professor Lionel Budden, who exercised the privilege, afforded to newly appointed professors, of making new appointments to their staffs with a view to developing such policies as seemed expedient in the circumstances. Some of the newcomers had drunk the heady wine, not so much of the Glory that was Greece and the Grandeur that was Rome, as of the left-wing student politics then fashionable at the British School at Rome and the French Ecole des Beaux Arts, which they appeared to believe were essential to the creation of good architecture.

By 1936 the Modern Movement was beginning to look almost respectable, and, just to make sure, Professor Pevsner provided it with a pedigree in his *Pioneers of the Modern Movement*, published in that year. Whether the pioneers would have acknowledged their alleged descendants is doubtful.

However, the Pioneers found themselves in competition for attention with happenings in the outside world: 1935 was the year of Mussolini's adventure into Abyssinia, and the question of sanctions was uppermost in the thoughts of the politically minded. Indeed we had a succession of anxious Septembers, culminating, after Munich in 1938, with Neville Chamberlain's tired and disillusioned voice, telling us over the radio, on the 3rd September, 1939, that we were at war with Germany. It was some time late in November that I found myself on my road to Damascus.

My home was in the Wirral, some twelve miles from Liverpool, and, having some time to spare before my tram was due to leave, I called at the University Club, on my way to the station, to look at the weekly papers over a cup of tea and a biscuit. When I entered the building it was still light outside. An hour or so later, not having previously experienced a 1939 style city black-out. I found myself

> Surrounded by a universal blank
> Of Nature's works to me expunged and rased
> And wisdom at one entrance quite shut out.
> So much the rather, thou Celestial Light,
> Shine inward, and the mind, through all its powers
> Irradiate. There plant eyes; all mist from thence
> Purge and disperse, that I may see and tell
> Of things invisible to mortal sight.

—lines to which I had not given a thought since, as a schoolboy, I had had to study the first three books of Milton's *Paradise Lost* as a set text in the School Certificate Examination.

From that moment in the black-out at the bottom of Mount Pleasant, Liverpool, I began to realize that I had been following, if any, a materialistic theory of architecture. I must go back to the beginning, and start again. The result, eventually, was that, as it now seems to me, the function of architecture, as distinct from mere building, is the ornamentation of cities, and, in special circumstances, landscapes. Now ornament is a form of praise, requiring its own special language and having its own vocabulary, grammar, rhetoric and logic. As such it cannot be invented at will. It must grow, and, as it grows, it gathers to itself the affections of those who use it with understanding.

Fortunately the conditions in a modern university during the war stimulated thought and fostered study. The numbers of undergraduates diminished as they were called up for national service, and a considerable number of senior members were seconded to government posts for the duration of the war. Those who remained had fewer calls upon their time. In my own case, having been rejected for military service, I was directed, when the Professor of Civic Design joined the Ministry of Town and Country Planning, to take charge of the Department of Civic Design, which carried with it the editorship of the *Town Planning Review*. My first duty, from then onwards, was to get copy for that journal. Here was an opportunity to kill two birds with one stone, by reading as much as I could of the classics of the theory of architecture, including such works as the *De Architectura* of Vitruvius and the *De Re Aedificatoria* of Leon Battista Alberti, both of which dealt with the planning of cities, and Ebenezer Howard's *Garden Cities of To-morrow* (edition of 1946 ed. F. J. Osborn], all of them books referred to in lectures though rarely read, even by the lecturers themselves. For the rest, I cannot say my reading ranged as widely as my ignorance was deep, but I hope widely enough for the immediate purpose. Indeed, I had some sympathy with the student who, when asked in an examination paper to define the limits of his subject, began: 'Town Planning is vast; indeed it is life itself.'

Perhaps that is why I deserted town planning at the first opportunity.

I must now return to the project shown in **Fig. 21.** It shows a block of flats of nine storeys, raised on stilts, in a rural setting, the idea being that a multi-storeyed building occupies less ground-space per standard unit of accommodation than one of fewer storeys, which would be a convenient way of helping to preserve the countryside. At the same time, however, it would necessarily transgress one of the timeless—and therefore inescapable—rules of architectural rhetoric: 'The bigger the building, the bigger the parts.' [Author's paraphrase of L. B. Alberti, *De Re Aedificatoria*, I ix]. If I take a Greek or Roman temple as the simplest example of the operation of the rule, it is not to suggest that we should build houses that look like Greek or Roman temples. I assume, however, that anybody with an interest in architecture will know what such temples look like; and, probably, know that the proportions of their parts were determined in accordance with customary rules that vary only slightly from building to building of the same order or style. The crucial feature is the door leading to the cella, which would, presumably, serve its utilitarian purpose if it were no more than, shall we say, two metres high and about half as much in width. If. however, we look at the Temple of Fortuna Virilis, which is amongst the smallest in Rome, we find that the height of the door opening is about 5.7 metres, and the width, three [H. Despouy, *Fragments d'Architecture Antique*, n.d. Pl. 50].

The late Sir Charles Reilly, when examining a student's project, had a habit of saying: 'Now let me see! We come in here' (pointing to the main entrance) 'and then what do we do?' As an undergraduate I used to think that this was no more than an intriguing little foible of his: it was a long time after I had graduated, and indeed, after I had left Liverpool for good, that what I had thought was a harmless habit actually embodied the first principles of architectural composition. When we approach an unfamiliar building for the first time we want to know, at a glance, where we go in. The building itself should tell us, in the same unequivocal manner as does the Temple of Fortuna Virilis —by the position and size of its entrance, approached through a prostyle porch, where we may pause to admire the richness of the ornament before we proceed to enter the house of a god. The arrangement is at once utilitarian and ceremonial, easily recognized and at the same time graciously welcoming. If, on the other hand, the door were of minimum size to admit an adult person, a man might feel, not only in doubt whether that door was the right one, but also that a man might have the impression that he could gain admission only by going down on all fours and crawling in.

The block of flats that was our starting-point (**Fig. 21**) belongs to a very different world from all this: it is quantitative rather than proportional, and although it was, and still is, claimed that, if we build high, more land is freed for open spaces, the law of proportion prevails in the end. The higher we build the more restricted an adjacent open space appears to be, and the men, women and children who live in the high-rise flats seem to have been reduced to the size of pigmies.

In his appendix W. A. Eden argues that the aesthetic failure of modern architecture is due to an increase in *size* of buildings not being accompanied by a corresponding increase in *scale*. In modern city planning the wide roads which cut broad swathes between tall buildings tend to enhance the barren effect. The buildings, because they are small in *scale* are not awe-inspiring but, because they are large, at the time dominate the city scene.

Now that you have read Units 21–22 perhaps you would like to consider whether these faults in any way undermine the validity of the Modern Movement philosophy. Are the faults inherent in the system, or do they only appear when the system is not handled with respect?

Acknowledgements

Grateful acknowledgement is made to the copyright holders for material used in these units:

Figures

1 from *The Plumber and Sanitary Houses*, Batsford, 1877; *2* from *Nature*, 1877 (Mary Evans Picture Library); *3* Post Office; *4 and 5* Reyner Banham, *Architecture of the Well-Tempered Environment*, Architectural Press, 1969; *6 Architectural Review*, Vol. 108, July–December 1950; *7* W. Shaw Sparrow, *Flats, Urban Houses and Cottage Homes*, Hodder, 1906; *8–12, 20–3 and 32* F. R. S. Yorke and F. Gibberd, *The Modern Flat*, Architectural Press, 1937; *13* RIBA *Journal*, May 1931 (GLC); *14* Shelvoke & Drewry Ltd; *15–17* RIBA *Journal*, 14 April 1934; *18* Magistrat der Stadt Wien, Plan und Schriftenkammer; *19 The Daily Worker*, 19 February 1934; *24* Moderne Bauformen, 1931; *25* W. Ingham Ashworth, *Flats: design and equipment*, Pitman, 1936; *26* Building Centre Committee, *Housing: a European Survey*, 1936; *27 and 28* Courtesy of Sir F. Gibberd; *29 and 30 Architect and Building News*, 15 January 1937; *31* Liverpool City Libraries.

Plates

1 and 2 United Nations; *3 and 4* Lucien Hervé; *5* G. E. Kidder Smith; *6, 17, 20, 23 and 29* from Reyner Banham, *Architecture of the Well-Tempered Environment*, Architectural Press, 1969; *7* Sandak; *8* Roger Viollet; *9, 24 and 26–8* Science Museum, London (Crown copyright); *10* Facsimile of first advertisement, *Journal of Gaslighting*, December 1890 (Institute of Gas Engineers); *11* E. R. Robson, *School Architecture*, 1874; *12* Mary Evans Picture Library; *13* Mansell Collection; *14* Radio Times Hulton Picture Library; *15* Hedrich-Blessing; *16* J. K. Freitag, *Architectural Engineering*, John Wiley, 1901; *18 and 19* Keith Gibson; *21* Glasgow School of Art; *22 and 68–72* Tim Benton; *30* Chicago Architectural Photographing Company; *31* William T. O'Dea, *The Social History of Lighting*, Routledge & Kegan Paul, 1958; *32* David Amy; *33* National Buildings Record; *34–5 and 42–3* Haden-Carrier Ltd; *36 and 44–5* BBC Copyright Photographs; *37* Bildarchiv Foto Marburg; *38–41* BBC Engineering Division; *46* London Transport Executive; *47–8, 55–7, 61–5 and 74–94* Stephen Bayley; *49 and 50* W. Shaw Sparrow, *Flats, Urban Houses and Cottage Homes*, Hodder, 1906; *51–2, 54 and 58* F. R. S. Yorke and F. Gibberd, *The Modern Flat*, Architectural Press, 1937; *53 Architectural Review*, LXXII, 1932; *59 and 60* GLC Photograph Library; *66 and 67* Photo: Paul Grünzweig; *73* Building Centre Committee, *Housing: a European Survey*, 1936.

History of architecture and design 1890–1939

Colour filmstrip illustrations associated with Units 21–22

1 Edward Maufe, Religous Services Studio, Broadcasting House, London (Architectural Review)
2 Dorothy Warren Trotter, Studio 3D, Broadcasting House, London (Architectural Review)
3 Wells Coates. Dramatic Control Room No. 1, Broadcasting House, London (Architectural Review)
4 Raymond McGrath, Vaudeville Studio, Broadcasting House, London (Architectural Review)
5 A corner of the central control room, Broadcasting House, London (Architectural Review)
6 W. H. Scrymgeour, Bickenhall Mansions, London W.1, 1896, view from Bickenhall Street (Stephen Bayley)
7 Frederick Gibberd, Ellington Court, Southgate, London, 1936, view from Southgate High Street (Stephen Bayley)
8 Maxwell Fry *et al.*, Kensal House, Ladbroke Grove, London, 1935, view from rear (Stephen Bayley)
9 Lancelot Herman Keay, St Andrew's Gardens, Liverpool, 1937, view of internal courtyard (Stephen Bayley)
10 Detail of parabolic arch (Stephen Bayley)
11 Connell, Ward and Lucas, Kent House, Kentish Town, London, 1936, view from Ferdinand Street (Stephen Bayley)
12 View from access galleries at rear (Stephen Bayley)

1

1 *Wallace K. Harrison, Secretariat Tower of the United Nations Building, general view, 1950, New York*

2	3
4	3
6	5

2 *Detail of façade showing short ends* **3** *Le Corbusier with Lucio Costa and Oscar Niemeyer, Ministry of Health and Education, detail, 1937–43, Rio de Janeiro* **4** *Le Corbusier, Project 23A, 1947* **5** *Ministry of Health and Education, detail of* brise-soleil **6** *Willis H. Carrier, United Nations Building, section of wall*

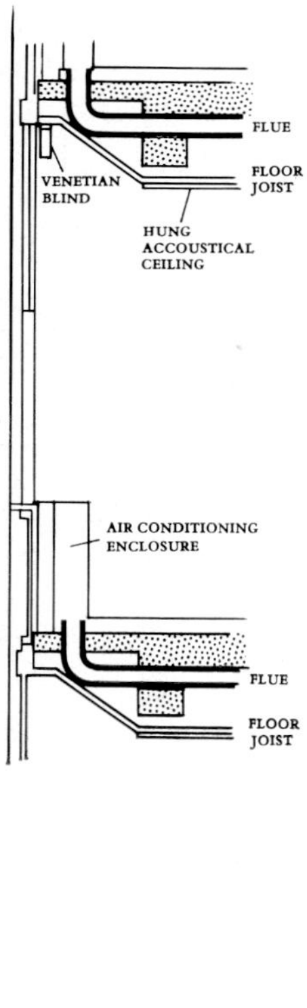

7	8
9	10
11	12

7 *Radio City, New York (Rockefeller Centre), 1931–40* 8 *Philippe Lebon, experimenter with coal-gas light, c. 1800* 9 *William Murdoch, coal-gas light, in his house at Redruth c. 1800* 10 *Auer von Welsbach, incandescent gas mantle, c. 1800* 11 *'Sunburner' lamp* 12 *Gasolier*

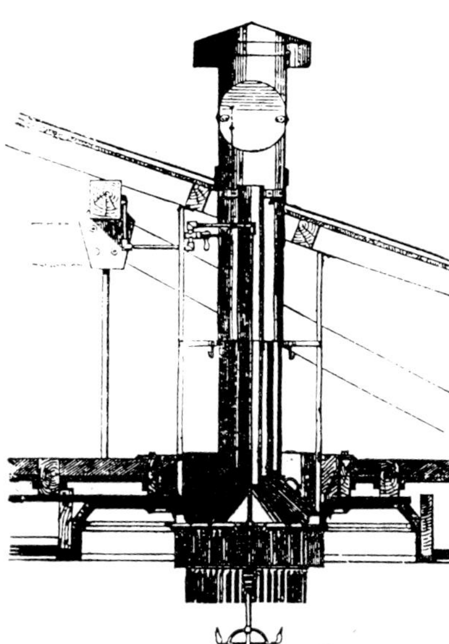

13
14

13 *18th century German traditional north European stove* **14** *American 'Franklin'-type stove—'The Anglo Saxon'*

15
16

15 *Holabird and Roche, Marquette Building, 1894, Chicago* **16** *Plan*

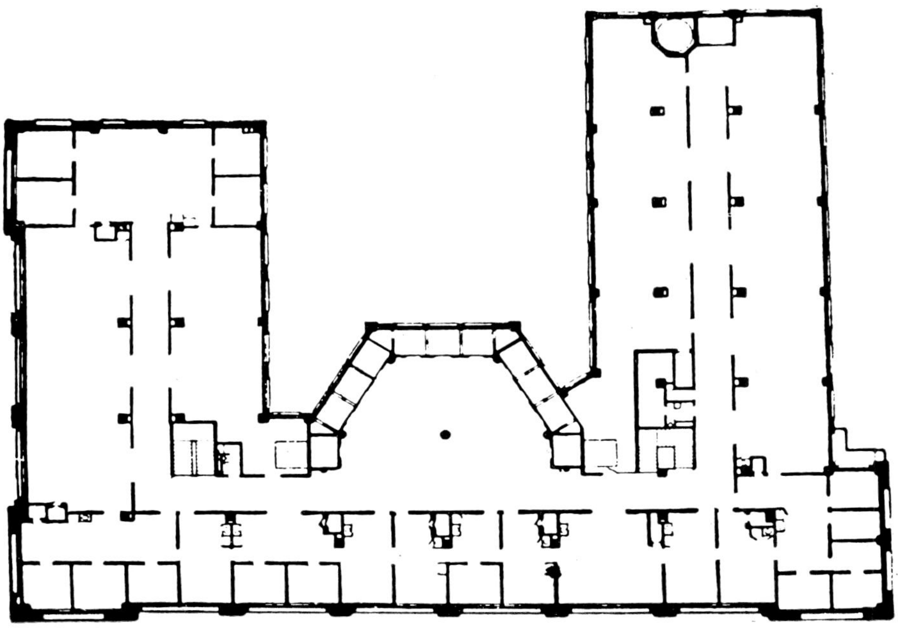

17a	18
17b	19

17 *John Hayward, draught-free house, 1867* **18** *Cuthbert Brodrick, Town Hall, exterior view showing ventilating ducts, 1863, Leeds* **19** *view, showing ducts*

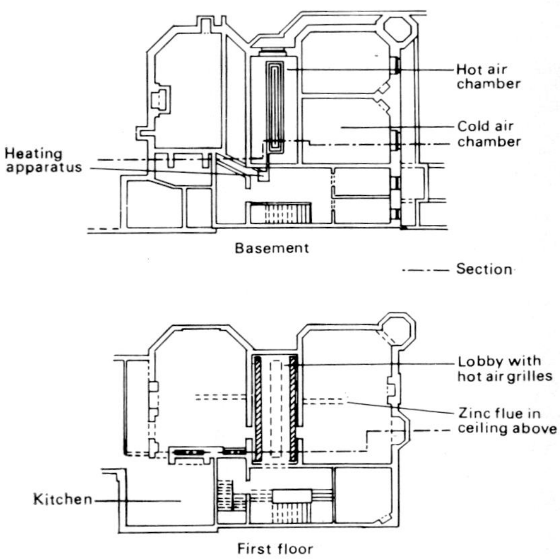

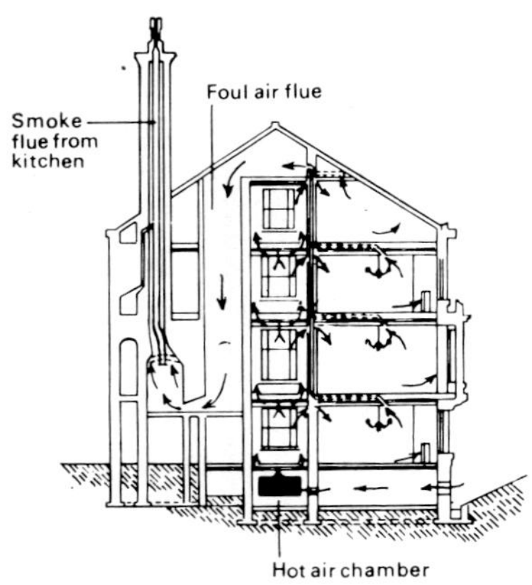

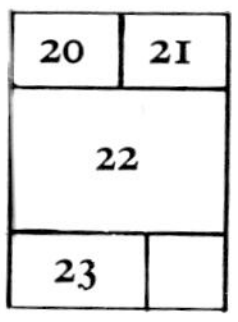

20 *Charles Rennie Mackintosh, School of Art, interior showing ventilation outlets, 1904, Glasgow* **21** *Plan, showing window bay in library* **22** *Lighting in the library* **23** *Henman and Cooper, the Royal Victoria Hospital, 1903, Belfast*

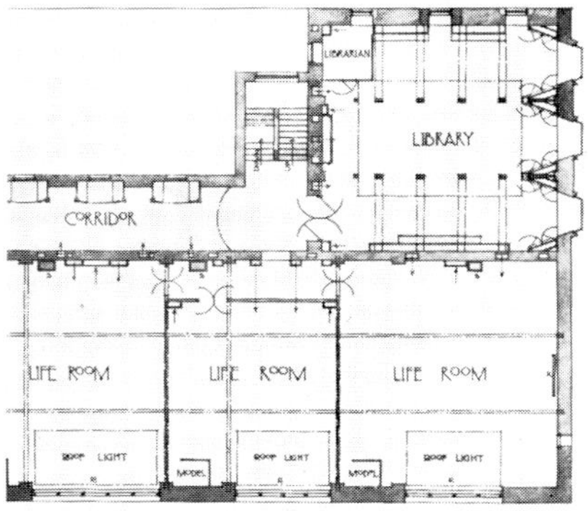

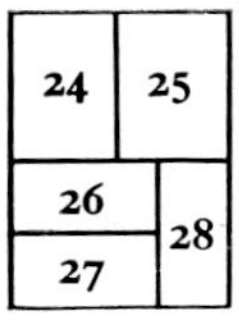

24 *Swann's early filament bulb* **25** *Jabocklov's arc lamp*
26 *Pearl Street Power Station (Edison), New York* **27** *Deptford Power Station (Ferranti), London* **28** *Thomas Alva Edison, electric light bulb*

29

30

29 *Frank Lloyd Wright, the Robie House, main first floor living room, section and plan, 1910, Chicago* **30** *Dining room, showing globe lights*

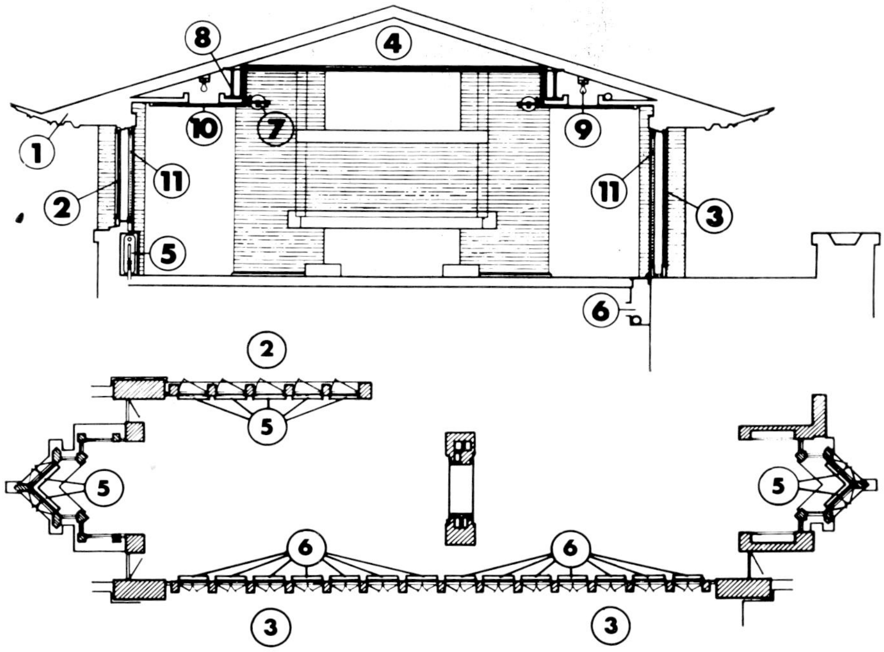

31 *Neon tubes on a pre-First World War London cinema* **32** *E. A. Stone, the Astoria Cinema, Finsbury Park, London plenum chamber, 1930* **33** *William Edward Trent, New Victoria Cinema, 1930, interior, London*

34 | 36
35 | 36
37

34 *Willis H. Carrier, 'Weathermaster' system, 1937* **35** *The Carrier Co. Ltd., miniaturized air-conditioning unit, 1939–1945* **36** *Val Myer, Broadcasting House, general view, 1932, London* **37** *Hans Poelzig, the Rundfunkhaus, general view, 1930, Berlin*

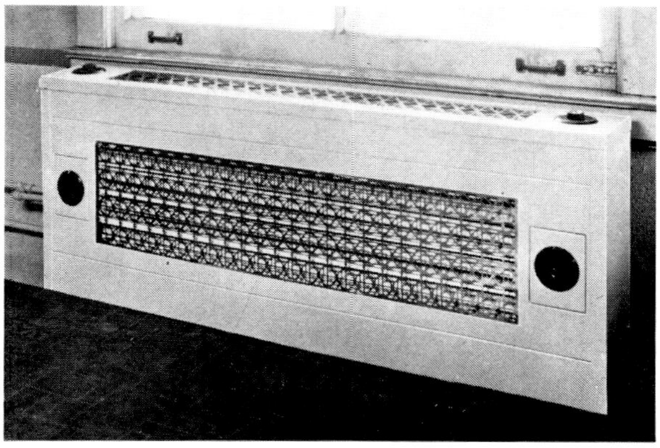

<table>
<tr><td>38</td><td>40</td><td>41</td></tr>
<tr><td colspan="2">39</td><td rowspan="2">44</td></tr>
<tr><td colspan="2">42</td></tr>
<tr><td colspan="2">43</td><td rowspan="2">45</td></tr>
<tr><td colspan="2">46</td></tr>
</table>

38 *Broadcasting House, corridor ceiling construction showing the method of sound-deadening the ventilation trunking* 39 *Foundations* 40 *Construction detail showing the structurally separate studio tower on the left* 41 *Ducts in a studio* 42 *Refrigerating equipment for studio air-conditioning plant* 43 *One of the fan motors of the concert hall air-conditioning equipment* 44 *Talks Studio* 45 *Religious Broadcasts Studio* 46 *London Transport, rolling stock on the Piccadilly Line*

47
48

47 *Henry Roberts, Model Dwellings for Families, general view, 1849, Bloomsbury, London* **48** *View of the access galleries*

49	50
51	52

49 *R. Norman Shaw, the Albert Hall Mansions, 1878, London* **50** *Edwin T. Hall, the Mansions, Sloane Gardens, plan, later nineteenth century* **51** *Closed flat plan of the nineteenth century* **52** *Open flat plan of the twentieth century (Lubetkin's and Tecton's Highpoint I)*

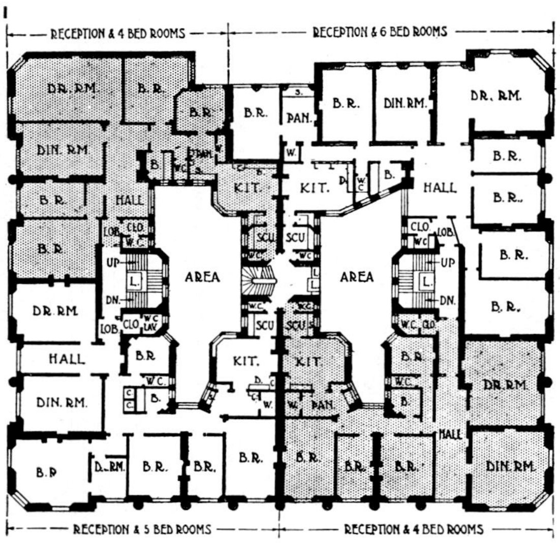

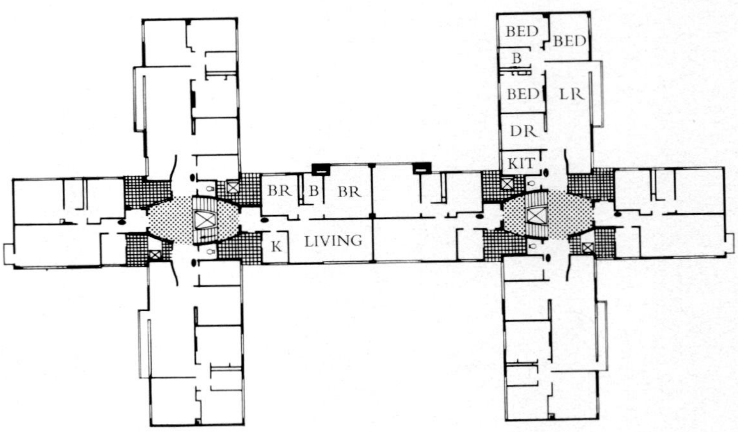

53

53 *Wells Coates, comparative illustrations of a flat decorated in a Victorian–Edwardian idiom and the same flat converted to 1930s taste*

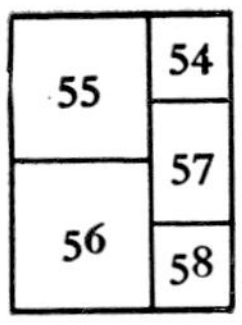

54 *Frederick Gibberd, Ellington Court, Southgate, interior, 1936, London* **55** *Wells Coates, the Isokon Flats, Hampstead, galleries from the rear, 1934, London* **56** *Galleries from the interior* **57** *Bathroom* **58** *Kitchen*

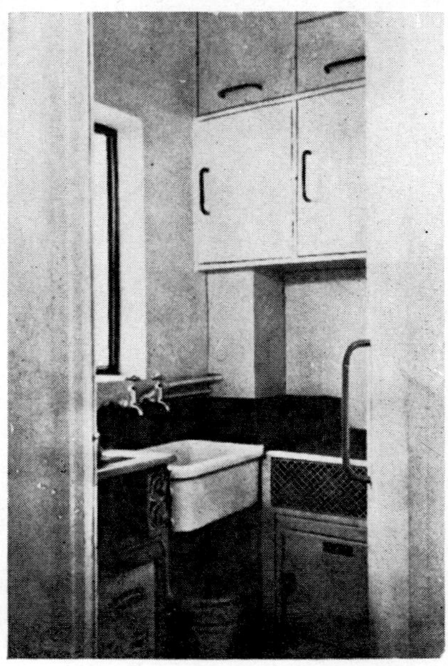

59
60

59 *L.C.C. Architect's Department, the Tabard Street Estate, general view, 1917, London* **60** *G. Topham Forrest, the East Hill Estate, Wandsworth*

61
62

61 *G. Topham Forrest and E. Haden Parkes, the Ossulston Estate, general view, 1928, St. Pancras, London* **62** *Internal corner*

63	
64	65

63 *General view* **64** *Detail of balconies* **65** *Detail of doorway*

66
67

66 *Dorfmeister, flats on the Döblinger Gürtel, general view, 1925, Vienna* **67** *Karplus, Dittes-Hof, general view, 1928, Vienna*

68	
69	70

68 *Karl Ehn, the Karl-Marx-Hof, 1927, Vienna* **69** *Detail* **70** *Detail*

71	
72	73

71 R. A. H. Livett, Quarry Hill, 1934–41, Leeds **72** *Detail* **73** *Plan*

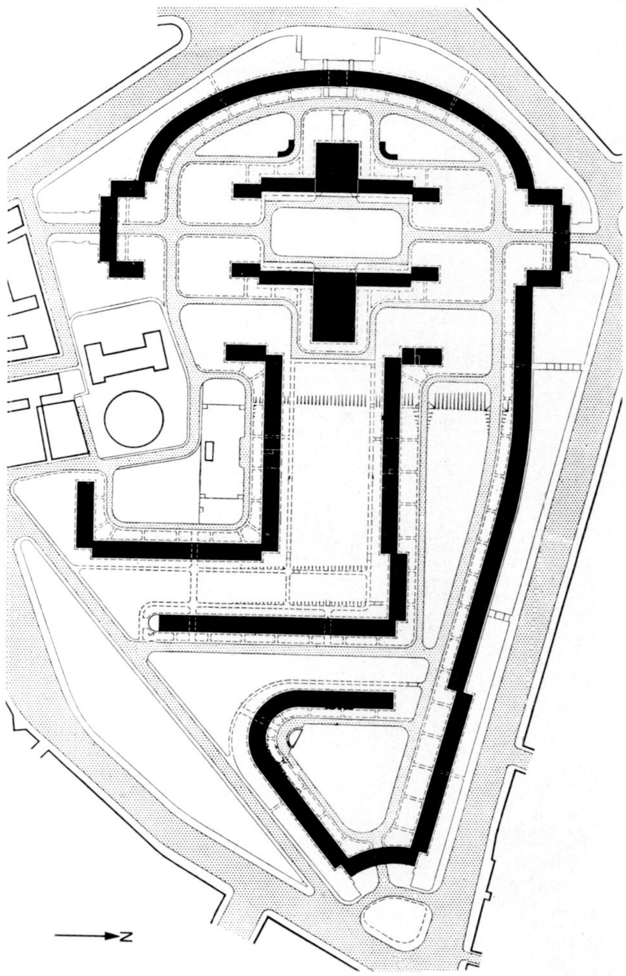

74

74 *Maxwell Fry et al., Kensal House, view from the street, 1935, Ladbroke Grove, London*

75
76

75 *A wing* **76** *A block*

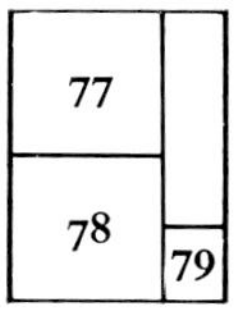

77 *Detail of balconies* **78** *Detail* **79** *Detail showing use of 4″ concrete*

80 *Frederick Gibberd, Ellington Court, view from the front, 1936, Southgate, London* **81** *View from the rear*
82 *Detail of doorway*

83 *Lancelot Herman Keay, St. Andrew's Gardens, view of entrance, 1937, Liverpool* **84** *Internal courtyard*
85 *Internal courtyard*

86 *Detail of galleries and stairwells* **87** *Detail of parabolic arch* **88** *View from Copperas Hill*

89

89 *Connell, Ward and Lucas, Kent House, view from Ferdinand Street, 1936, Kentish Town, London*

90

90 *Connell, Ward and Lucas, Kent House, another view*

91
92

91 *Staircase* **92** *Staircase*

93

94

93 *Internal Courtyard* **94** *Detail of balconies*